WORK, WOMEN AND THE STRUGGLE FOR SELF-SUFFICIENCY

The **WIN** Experience

Aliki Coudroglou

UNIVERSITY
PRESS OF
AMERICA

Library of Congress Cataloging in Publication Data

Coudroglou, Aliki.
   Work, women, and the struggle for self-sufficiency.

   Bibliography: p.
   Includes index.
   1. Work Incentive Program--Arizona--Phoenix. I. Title.
HD5726.P53C6 1982   362.5'84'09791   82-13679
ISBN 0-8191-2654-3
ISBN 0-8191-2655-1 (pbk.)

To the memory of my parents

Acknowledgements

This work has been long in the making. A personal interest in the struggle of women for economic independence, and long professional association with mothers dependent on public assistance, found their first expression in the doctoral requirements for a dissertation. That experiment served as a stimulus to explore the world of work, and the potential of training programs to provide people who had been excluded from social institutions with the means of entering the mainstream of society. My thanks go to Dr. Sheila Akabas of Columbia University School of Social Work, whose work in Industrial Social Welfare has demonstrated the wealth of opportunity for research and service in the work arena. Her scholarship and personal enthusiasm have supported my curiosity in the social policy and service dimensions of the occupational world.

I should also like to acknowledge my indebtedness to Emogene Brayer and Ruby Morris, retired and present managers of the Phoenix WIN office respectively, and their staffs, for their generosity of spirit, time and resources.

Sincere appreciation is extended to the WIN enrollees, past and present, without whose cooperation, of course, this study could have never been completed.

Besides the learning it has provided for me, this study has helped me realize that I have many friends who care for me and have invested in me. This realization alone was worth the effort for this study. Particularly, I wish to recognize the valuable support of my friend Ruth Wootten and colleague Dr. Dennis Poole for their willingness to read the manuscript and provide critical and editorial comments; my colleague Dr. Darrel Montero for believing in the value of my work and encouraging my pursuing its publication; Donna Smith, Kay Cochlin and Betty Wood, members of the clerical staff of the School of Social Work of Arizona State University, for their enthusiastic assistance with typing, xeroxing and all those supportive tasks that make the work of a researcher bearable; my students Sheila Garos and Sharon Stephens

v

for their help in preparing the index; and Margaret Heath and her staff in the secretarial pool, particularly Barbara Bellamy, for their taking such a personal interest in this manuscript.

A year of sabbatical leave has been spent in preparing this book. However, I doubt whether I would have been able to carry this project through without the support of these friends and colleagues.

TABLE OF CONTENTS

LIST OF TABLES

CHAPTER I

INTRODUCTION

Among public enterprises perhaps none has been assigned higher hopes and financial investments than manpower training. Conceptualized as tools for developing human resources, manpower programs have been seen both as means of saving public expenditures and of restoring human dignity to those dependent on public support. Yet these programs are now under tremendous criticism for their failure to stop the drain on the public budget caused by the economic dependency of those hard-to-employ. At time of economic pressures, such as these we face today, there is strong protest against the deployment of public expenditures, particularly in the field of welfare. While serving the "truly needy" remains an acknowledged administrative responsibility, the current political mood of fiscal conservationism clearly mandates that "one's upkeep" is one's own liability.

This message came very early to the Work Incentive Program.* Established in 1967, the program has sought to put people in Aid to Families with Dependent Children (AFDC) to work. As these families consisted primarily of women with minor children, the program actually addresses the employability of welfare mothers. Initially, a variety of educational and training services were provided, with participants spending often more than a year in the program. Soon, however, education and training were reduced. The program's current concentration is on immediate job placement, often with on-the-job training provisions.

WIN has some unique features that set it apart from other training programs. Administrative responsibilities, for instance, are shared by two departments: Labor, and Health and Human Services. The program also deals exclusively with recipients of public assistance, specifically those in the AFDC category. Most importantly, however, the program was initiated to develop the employability of women dependent on welfare. Whatever that means regarding the public's attitudes toward these women, the program signals the

---

*Hereafter to be referred to as WIN.

1

social trend of women's march into the labor market and demonstrates the struggle that this trend entails.

Background Issues

The Work Incentive Program was authorized by the 1967 Amendments of the Social Security Act. Even before its inception WIN had stirred great controversy. Designed "to respond vigorously and effectively to the changing manpower needs of our society"[1] the program has alarmed many by its potential for coercion in pursuing the "vigorous" part of its goals, while others have been concerned about the limitations to its "effectiveness." The ambiguous premises of the WIN program are evidenced even in official testimonies. For instance, while the WIN staff are advised "to be prepared to deal with hostility to the WIN program because of its punitive implications,"[2] former Secretary Hodgson contended that "WIN has an inadequate penalty for refusing work . . . (and) . . . a faulty referral process . . . left to the discretion of the State Welfare agencies."[3]

Basic in the WIN controversy is the question regarding the right-to-welfare and/or right-to-work of poor people. Is the primary goal of a work incentive program to relieve the manpower needs of society, to assist disadvantaged individuals to gain emotional uplifting and financial independence, or to weed out the social parasites from the deserving poor? These goals do not, of course, have to be self-contradictory. But the emphasis in orientation will no doubt highlight the priorities given in the implementation of the program. Subsequently, its effectiveness must be evaluated on the basis of expressed goals at the service level.

Another side of the same problem is whether people should be supported by welfare or should be made to work for their maintenance. When former President Nixon signed his "workfare" legislation[4] on December, 1971, he stated that "it is the sweat and labor of generations past and present that have brought us where we are today, that have piled high the wealth that enables us to be among the most generous nations in history."[5] The irony of his argument notwithstanding, the key message here is that self-development comes by the sweat of one's labor, while--quoting again former President Nixon in his invocation of F.D.R during the same affair--"continued dependence on relief induces a spiritual and moral disintegration fundamentally destructive to the national fiber."[6] In the same ideological vein, a panelist at a professional meeting introduced a discussion on the work ethic by stating that this ethic "has been based on the theory that human beings naturally want to work,"[7] while an experiment undertaken by the Office of Economic Opportunity showed that "work incentive doesn't take a nose dive even when there are income guarantees."[8]

To posit the question more bluntly, is the "work ethic" invoked here a mere political tool to save the government money, a feasible vehicle to help individuals out of a financial cul-de-sac, or a meaningful principle that involves and affects one's total makeup beyond and above one's ability to be self-supporting? In short, what are we really trying to accomplish through the WIN program and how can we best accomplish it? Again the question becomes one of orientation to the program and of the priorities emphasized in its implementation. And, as in the evaluation of all such programs, it is only the reference to its objectives that success can be measured. That is, the results of WIN should be assessed in terms of the degree of realization of its objectives.

One of the explicit WIN objectives is to assist those enrolled in the program to achieve "independence and useful roles in the communities."[9] As Dubey and his colleagues indicate, "WIN is a continuation of the American welfare effort through work relief. . . . Its antecedents are the WPA and other depression-rooted programs."[10] However, unlike the programs of the 1930's, WIN "was conceived as a response to economic growth rather than the depression, and to the changing composition and general growth of the Aid to Families with Dependent Children program."[11]

As the social conditions that gave rise to the WIN program, and the population for which WIN was created, are different than previous work relief efforts, it is legitimate to assume that WIN's ideological base--and thus its interpretation--could differ in essence, although its articulation is similar. Smarr and Escoll, for instance, claim that the old work ethic was "a result, and only secondarily a cause [of American economic progress], and its role in history must change as society changes."[12] They explain that "the 'good old work ethic' worked because new frontiers of geography, and then industry, were created by the

3

efforts of Renaissance, and we have been in its fall-
out ever since. But no longer are frontiers of
opportunity expanding. The very product of that
history, 'the developed society,'. . . makes [some
categories of people] superfluous unless they aspire
only to continue the status quo."[13]

It was basically an effort to change the financially
depressed status of a large and mixed population that
prompted the work relief programs of the 1930's. But
in the present time a "change in the status quo" may
not necessarily mean a financial change, or at least
not only that. Ours--and WIN's--has been a time of
civil rights movement, of minority consciousness
raising, of concepts of equity and maximum feasible
participation, and even of plans for the greening of
America. The social reforms of the 1960's have sensi-
tized a social awareness that seeks the development of
not only one's purchasing power but one's living capability as well. One may, then, interpret the choice
of stating the WIN objective mentioned earlier in
terms of "restoring . . . such individuals to independence and useful lives in their communities," as
implying a broader conceptualization of the work
ethic. As Cox states, "the values of employment (especially for AFDC mothers) are in self-respect, good
example for the children, opportunity to join in the
mainstream of American life and the like, rather than
in the mother's earning capacity."[14] If such an
orientation to the WIN's goals is accepted administratively, the program's implementation will more likely
emphasize activity that fosters the quality of its
clients, not merely their financial leverage.

One WIN provision directly affecting such activity is
the provision of supportive services. Also referred
to as "counseling," "coaching," "guidance," "social
services," or "follow-through," supportive services
are an integral part of the program. Their importance
lies in their everpresence, so to speak, or rather in
the possibility of their everpresence. They begin
when the enrollee enters the program and continue
until the enrollee no longer holds this status. Such
services relate to the activities of all team members
and penetrate all WIN components. As the directives
of the WIN Technical Assistance Book indicate, they
"should be available wherever the enrollee needs them
whenever he needs them."[15] The WIN supportive services describe less a specific activity than "a
commitment and a stubborn preoccupation" aiming at

4

assisting the enrollee in 'making it.'"[16] It is perhaps this very nature of the supportive services that
has caused the controversy around their provision.
Although official reports indicate that "almost every
element of the (WIN) program has been disappoint-
ing,"[17] no other WIN aspect has received as hard a
lash by the WIN revisionist measures as the provision
of supportive services. While WIN I--as the original
WIN legislation has come to be known--gave supportive
services a prominent role in the WIN program, explicitly assigning them to all technical activities,[18]
proponents of WIN II philosophy--Talmadge Amendments
and after--consider them some sort of psychological
pampering representing the interests of the giver
rather than receiver.[19] Their virtual elimination by
subsequent legislation testifies to their controversy.[20]

Changes in the 1971 legislation called for: mandatory
registration of all individuals on AFDC rolls for
manpower services unless specifically exempted; a
shift in emphasis from preparation for work to job
placement; closer coordination between the two administering agencies--the Departments of Labor and of
Health, Education and Welfare (now Health and Human
Services); and controlled, on-going evaluation of the
program's effectiveness. The legislation imposed
specific administrative and structural requirements on
the program to meet these objectives. It also provided tax credits to employers of WIN trainees in order
to stimulate local job market opportunities. There
has been no significant change in the WIN provisions
since then.

It is evident from the above that the current WIN
policy reflects the government's determination to
reduce welfare rolls and costs through a stricter,
more visible work-oriented WIN activity. However,
there has been no foundation that a change in the
functional ecology of the delivery of service will
bring about the desired outcome of lasting employment
for a population like the one served by WIN. Indeed
there has been little attention given to the delivery
of such important a component as the supportive
services. Despite a generous budget for research
authorized by the Department of Labor, and the great
volume of resulted studies, it has not yet been established just what aspects of the trainees' experience
are responsible for helping them with their training
effort.[21] It appears that policy decisions regarding
the provision of services have been made arbitrarily

5

with the mandate on emphasizing or eliminating them from the WIN program depending entirely on ideological orientation rather than empirical assessments.

It is unfortunate that a federally funded manpower program designed to enhance the employability of those not adequately prepared for job market competition could have continued for more than a decade with little knowledge of the specific nature of transactions at the level of service delivery. How are supportive services influencing the enrollees' involvement in their training? To what extent do they contribute to one's engagement in the program? How are supportive services best delivered? What skills are needed for their delivery?

This lack of concrete information is particularly disturbing since it comes at a time when groups of people--such as the disabled, displaced homemakers, deinstitutionalized long-term patients of mental hospitals--are pressing for their right to employability and self-sufficiency. Having been systematically excluded from gainful employment and with a long history of social dependency, these individuals seek their restoration to a respected status which inheres in one's occupational role. Knowing how to help them reach this role is, therefore, imperative.

Parameters of the Study

The purpose of this study is to assess whether supportive services do indeed play an essential role in an enrollee's success in the WIN program. To this end a survey has been undertaken of the Phoenix WIN office enrollees--those who terminated their training successfully and those who dropped out--and of the WIN staff, comparing their perceptions of the nature of supportive services offered in the program. The attempt has been to identify distinctive patterns in these services which are conducive to the successful completion of the enrollee's employability plans. These patterns have been sought in the hope of developing a more adequate understanding of factors that assist individuals with a history of economic and social dependency to alter their predicaments. Policy considerations, training modalities, as well as guidelines for staff preparation may then evolve as a result of such understanding.

The choice of the Phoenix office for such a study was prompted by an "end-of-the-month status" report of the national WIN activities for August 1971. In this report it was shown that while the national level of "completed job entry"--that is, successful termina- tion--was 4.1%, the Phoenix office's was a 5.2%, and while the rate of Indirect Job Entry--that is, after WIN services--for the nation in general was 10.4%, that for the Phoenix office was 19.9%.[22]

The report is significant for many reasons. First, this is virtually the last report available before the 1971 Social Security Amendments went into effect. As stated earlier, these amendments changed the emphasis of the program and eliminated the provision of suppor- tive services. The report indicates that the rate of success was greater after the intervention of sup- portive services; an indication that suggests that services may have a positive influence on the outcome of one's training.

Most important, though, the almost double rate of success of the Phoenix office is remarkable in view of the area's pioneer background and frontier quality. The city's vital statistics show tremendous growth from year to year, and comparisons with other large cities indicate that its cost of living is still relatively low. For instance, in 1971--the year of the above report--Phoenix[23] was 22nd among 25 selected cities, requiring only $10,454 yearly income for an urban family of four[24] to maintain an "intermediate living standard." Yet, less than 40% of the Phoenix families were able to afford this living, and of those who could not, approximately 50% had half the needed budget.[25] More[26] than 10% of families were below the poverty line, and of those, more than 30% had at least one fully-employed member in the household. To make the picture more complete, 21% of those families with below $5,000 yearly income relied on two or more jobs in the household in order to maintain this income.[27] Actually, Phoenix is a city of multiple-job households, with almost half of all households relying on two or more jobs to attain their income level. The 1971 percentage of those needing two or more jobs to[28] attain the $10,000-and-over income bracket was 42%.

It should be noted that the choice of the year for the given data is made because of its relevance to this study. The 1980 income profile is essentially the same, although different in absolute numbers. Phoenix still ranks 22nd among 25 metropolitan areas in cost of living. However, now the amount needed for the same family to secure the same "intermediary" standard is $21,844.[29] With a reported median income of $21,933,[30] still less than 40% of the Phoenix population is able to enjoy that standard. The number of households below, or at the fringes of, the poverty level has increased to 18%.[31] More than 37% of households earning less than $10,000 a year relied on more than one job for their income.[32] While there is a steady increase in per capita personal income, Arizonans averaged $8,791 in 1980, compared with the U.S. average of $9,521.[33] That ranks the state as the 32nd in the nation.

It is evident that jobs do not pay well in Arizona, at least not as a general rule. But neither does public welfare. An HEW Trend report for July 1971 indicates that, although the amount of assistance needed for a family of four in Arizona, and to which such a family had been considered entitled, was $256 monthly, only $167 was paid, that is only 65% of the estimated need.[34] Actually, this "65% of the estimated need"-- the official basis for all public welfare payments--is a basic welfare philosophy of the Arizona legislature, one that yearly efforts by various interested groups have not managed to really break through.[35] As of other forms of welfare assistance, Arizona is equally restrictive as it has been evidenced by the resistance to conform with federal standards, thus having the dubious honor of being the only state in the Union to appeal to the Supreme Court the District Court of Appeals decision of proven non-conformity with the[36] Social Security Act.

It is true that Phoenix is a continuously growing city. Its population is increasing rapidly and its job market has enjoyed a tremendous expansion. Recently, however, the rate of job increase has slowed down significantly. The State's present unemployment rate is 6.7%.[37] Construction and government are[38] reported to be the weakest sectors of the economy. Despite the fact that metropolitan Phoenix contains 63% of the state's non-agricultural employment, the city's unemployment rate is 5.5%.[39] As 55% of the state's population live in the area, Phoenix is usually able to get the largest proportion of new jobs. Most of these jobs are in manufacturing, the sector that has the healthiest expansion rate.

The above trends have been in the making for sometime. A 1972 report, for instance, indicated that job opportunities had increased in [40] every field except in construction and agriculture. Yet, in the Phoenix area there was a 6.4% growth in the job market during 1971.[41] Then, even more than now, job increases were in areas that did not significantly affect women, at least not the women who enrolled in the WIN program. For instance, although there was about a 7.3% increase in manufacturing jobs, these jobs were mostly in the machinery category and in the electronics industry. Other high increases were in mining, contract construction, and trade categories.[42] These are not industries usually known for high levels of female employment. In December, 1971, for instance, the highest demand for workers was in the following jobs: automobile service station attendant, busboy, cook, cosmetologist, counterman, deliveryman, guard, handbill passer, janitor, kitchen helper, nurse's aid, nurse, general salesman, secretary, telephone solicitor, waiter/waitress, and in that order.[43]

From the above it is easy to conclude that there are very few well-paid job opportunities in Phoenix for women that have little education and limited or no skills. A "good job" in terms of adequate pay, requires considerable ability and time, and the training for it is long and demanding--much too long and much too demanding to be accommodated by the WIN provisions. There are, too, several contextual factors which further inhibit WIN's implementation in Phoenix. Public transportation, for one, is extremely limited and distances are tremendous as Phoenix is spread over 9,238 square miles of land,[44] much of it still unbuilt, desert, mountainous, or even farmland. Thus owning a car is a basic necessity of Arizona living.

Although there is an "inner city" area,[45] not all people on welfare are concentrated within its boundaries. Actually, there are no ghettoes in Phoenix in the strict sense of the word.[46] Chicanos, for instance, are spread throughout the metropolitan area, as are other minority and low income groups. Places of business, industry, services--any possible job resource--are also widespread, thus making the problem of transportation more serious.

Just as serious is the question of day care centers. Organized child care is a rather new idea in Phoenix and was certainly too novel in 1971. This is not in reference to the quality of day care centers, but

9

rather to their limited number, a problem that is accentuated by the issues of distances and transportation discussed above.

As there are no Medicaid[47] provisions in Arizona, the only places providing health care for the welfare poor are the county hospitals. There is only one such facility in Maricopa County and its accessibility is as problematic as that of the day care centers. The same is valid for the schools or other services one might need. One can very easily visualize a WIN mother waiting for 50-60 minutes for a bus in order to take her child to the day care center; then waiting another 50-60 minutes for another bus in order to get to the WIN office; and repeat the process in reverse in the evening. All these without including walking time to the bus stops--often not a negligible distance--or possible trips to her child's school, or a clinic, or even shopping.

The impression is that a "welfare" mother must be given enough satisfactions from the WIN experience to be able to bear with the difficulties of attaining this experience. In order to be successful, the compensations of the program must outweigh the hardships of the effort. If the WIN statistical reports indicated such a high rate of success, then . . . they must have done something right in Phoenix.

This study has been undertaken in order to understand the system of the delivery of WIN I services in the Phoenix WIN office. While the assessment is recent, the period assessed has, by choice, been one when supportive services were available, as these services form the core of the study. There is merit to this quest. Comparative studies of WIN I and WIN II[48] show that, although WIN II has been placing more persons in jobs, WIN I graduates obtain higher paying jobs and hold them longer. As of now, we do not know the "why" of this difference. The aim of this follow-up study is to assess whether supportive services--a yet unexplored field--contribute to the answer.

Content of the Book

The following chapter provides an analytical discourse of existing literature on the WIN program and issues related to it. The discussion provides the bases for the theoretical considerations that gave rise to the study. CHAPTER 3 explains the rationale, design, and methodology of this research project. The findings of the scheduled questionnaire are discussed in CHAPTER 4, while the analysis of the open-ended interviews is presented in CHAPTER 5. The conclusions of the study are drawn in the last chapter where a novel conceptual framework is introduced, one that hopefully fosters our understanding of the needs of those struggling for self-sufficiency.

FOOTNOTES

CHAPTER I

1. <u>WIN - Technical Assistance Book</u>, prepared by the Office of Human Resources Development and Training Operations of the U.S. Employment Service (November 1968), p. 1.

2. Ibid., p. 47.

3. Testimony of the Secretary of Labor, James D. Hodgson, before the Senate Finance Committee, July 29, 1971, U.S. Senate, Finance Committee, Social Security Amendments of 1971, CIS (1971 S361-10.3, pp. 128-186), p. 133.

4. Social Security Act Amendments (Talmadge Amendments), Sections 3, 85 Stat. 803 (1971), (PL-92-223 which makes registration with the manpower agency a condition for eligibility for AFDC).

5. <u>The New York Times</u>, December 29, 1971.

6. Ibid.

7. G. Scherberg, "The Work Ethic," Paper presented at the 50th Annual Meeting of American Orthopsychiatric Association, New York, June 1, 1973, mimeographed.

8. D. Kershaw, <u>The Arizona Republic</u>, March 26, 1973.

9. Social Security Act Amendments to Title IV, Part C., Section 204, 81 Stat. 884 (1968). (PL90-248).

10. S. Dubey, et al., "Structural Factors in Non-Compliance in Referring Clients to Programs in a Large Public Welfare Agency," in <u>The WIN Program</u>

11

Project: Preliminary Report, Cleveland, Ohio: School of Social Sciences, Case Western Reserve University (August 1970), mimeographed, Ch. I., p. 1.

11. Ibid.

12. E. Smarr and P. Escoll, "Humanism and the American Work Ethic, A Psycho-Social Perspective," Paper presented at the 50th Annual Meeting of American Orthopsychiatric Association, New York (June 1, 1973), p. 7. Mimeographed.

13. Ibid.

14. I. Cox, "The Employment of Mothers as a Means of Family Support," Welfare in Review, 8:6 (November-December 1970), p. 9.

15. WIN - Technical Assistance Book, op. cit., p. 69.

16. Ibid., pp. 69-70.

17. Report to Senate Finance Committee by the Library of Congress' Legislative Reference Service. Quoted in John Hamilton, "Will 'Work' Work?," Saturday Review (May 23, 1970), p. 25.

18. See directions in the WIN Administrative Manual regarding all WIN components. Also see directions in WIN Technical Assistance Book.

19. D. Moynihan, for instance, refers to such provisions as a "services strategy . . . one that seeks to make up presumed deficits in the behavior of one set of persons by providing them the counsel, advice and example of another set of persons with presumed surplus of such behavior. . . . The terms of the trade are, in essence, advice in return for deference." D. Moynihan, "One Step We Must Take," Saturday Review (May 23, 1970), p. 21. See also "The Allied Services Act of 1972," proposed by President Nixon in May 18, 1972. 18 Congressional Record H4685 (H. Doc. No. 296).

20. The Social Security Amendments of 1971 (PL 92-223) and the Revenue Sharing Act of 1972 (PL 92-512).

21. United States Department of Labor. The Work In-
    centive (WIN) Program and Related Experience. R
    & D Monograph 49 (1977), p. 2.

22. End-of-the-Month Report. Department of Labor
    Manpower Development Programs, WIN Cumulative
    Report (August 31, 1971).

23. By Phoenix, we refer to the larger metropolitan
    area which includes the entire Maricopa County.
    This is actually the area served by the Phoenix
    WIN office.

24. Valley National Bank, Arizona Statistical Review,
    28th Annual Edition (September 1972), p. 7. Note
    that the choice of the year for these and the
    following data is made because of its relevance
    to this study.

25. Ibid. It is interesting to note that the 1971
    median income of Metro Phoenix was $9,856.

26. Ibid., p. 6.

27. Ibid., p. 7.

28. Ibid.

29. Valley National Bank, Arizona Progress (July-
    August 1981), p. 2. The source given by all
    cities, except Phoenix, is the United States De-
    partment of Labor. Phoenix data are by Bureau of
    Business and Economic Research, College of Busi-
    ness Administration, Arizona State University,
    sponsored by Valley National Bank.

30. Inside Phoenix 1981. Phoenix Newspapers, Inc.,
    p. 3. Foresight Eighty, a survey of the Western
    Savings and Loan Association of Arizona reports
    median of $17,888 for metropolitan Phoenix. This
    makes even darker the economic picture of the
    area's low income people. Quoted in Arizona
    Poverty Profile, 1980, p. 36.

31. Ibid.

32. Ibid., p. 29.

33. The Arizona Republic, August 10, 1981.

13

34. Trend Report. Graphic Presentation of Public Assistance and Related Data. Department of HEW, Publication No. (SRS) 73-03101, NCSS Report A-4 (1971), p. 23.

35. The present level is 70% of the need.

36. Arizona has repeated incidents of not conforming with administrative standards. The one mentioned has to do with Arizona's refusal to honor federal conditions regarding residency; the recommendations of statewide advisory committee on child welfare services; computation of earnings and deduction of benefits; and guardianship of a child residing outside of the home of his ADC receiving mother. Note that Arizona still considers the program one addressed to the children alone, thus the ADC designation.

37. Arizona Progress, op. cit., p. 4.

38. Ibid., p. 1.

39. Ibid., p. 4.

40. Valley National Bank Statistical Review, 1972, op. cit.

41. Inside Phoenix, 1972, p. 28.

42. Ibid.

43. Ibid., p. 30. Note that the official wage rates were from $1.00 to $1.60 per hour or $30 - $70 weekly.

44. Arizona Blue Book 1971-72. Guide to the State of Arizona, Arizona State Library Association, p. 89.

45. The one known as "South Phoenix."

46. Unless, of course, we characterize as such the Indian Reservations, four of which are within Maricopa County, occupying 16% of its land area. (These Reservations are: Salt River, Fort McDowell, and Gila River. Also part of Papago.)

47. Medicaid legislation passed in 1974. However, because of intergovernmental complications no

funds have yet been allocated and no service has
been implemented.

48. B. R. Schiller, et al., <u>The Impact of WIN II; A
Longitudinal Evaluation</u>, Washington Pacific Consultants (1976).

CHAPTER II

THEORETICAL ISSUES AND PERSPECTIVES

There are many factors affecting a program like WIN. For a thorough understanding, the discussion addresses the following areas thought of as pertinent to the nature of this study:
- A. The WIN Program in its implementation
- B. WIN as a policy of social welfare
- C. Manpower issues
- D. Work ethic
- E. Characteristics of AFDC recipients
- F. Socio-psychological consequences of poverty
- G. Delivery of social services
- H. Organizational issues.

The WIN Program in its Implementation

A WIN research program, authorized by the same legislation that created the WIN manpower program, was launched in mid-1969. Its function was "to assist policymakers as they decide among alternatives by casting light not only on public areas in the WIN program itself but also on issues involved in major welfare reform."[1]

As the areas to which the above studies have been addressed are broad and relate to all the concerns of this study, only a descriptive review of their nature and findings will be given here. The theoretical considerations of their conclusions will be discussed in other parts of this chapter.

Perhaps the best known among the WIN studies is Leonard Goodwin's Do the Poor Want to Work?. In this he examines the work orientation of working and non-working poor, welfare recipients and non-recipients, WIN participants and non-participants: some 4,000 people in total. Goodwin defines "work orientations" as "psychological attributes that significantly influence activity in the world of work."[2] These attributes are basically: one's attitude toward work--what one expects to achieve through work; one's beliefs about one's ability to reach one's goals through work; and one's intention to secure income through work or through some other ways and means.[3] His findings are of significance mostly because they

17

give enough evidence to disperse the common anti-welfare myths. With reference to the welfare mothers, Goodwin found no difference in the work orientations of these mothers and working non-welfare people. There seemed to be no difference, even if the mothers have been long-term recipients. AFDC mothers seemed to have the same aspirations for a good life, which includes having a job. They seemed to share the middle-America ethic that work is contributing to their self-development. Although some difference was observed between the recipients' acceptance of governmental support and the resistance to such support by non-welfare poor, Goodwin found positive correlation between self-development orientation and high acceptance of support. He ascribes this acceptance tendency to the insecurity the welfare mother feels about her ability to achieve job success. He says: "Positive association of the work ethic with lack of confidence seems to characterize those who have failed, or are risking failure, in the work world."[4] This failure risk, the uncertainty about making it, Goodwin found, was a significant factor to the WIN enrollees. He found that "while employed terminees [of WIN] might well be expected to express less dependency and more self-confidence, the successful work experience has not led to changes in these orientations, according to the data. This essential stability, however, is a marked contrast to the increased dependency and lack of confidence of those who remained without jobs."[5] Another interesting finding of Goodwin, very relevant to the present study, is that, while there were no value differences between the welfare and non-welfare population with respect to work, welfare workers felt that such differences existed.

Another study, undertaken by Roessner, explained the thesis that in the world of work there are two partially contradictory value systems: that of employers and that of disadvantaged job seekers. These systems confront one another within the world of the job market.[6] Roessner and his associates hypothesized that "this potential clash of styles and values, coupled with the mutual needs of employer and disadvantaged job seeker, implies that accommodations must be made by employer, potential employee, or both in order that successful integration into the work situation can occur."[7] With a population consisting of some 300 WIN enrollees who were placed in jobs and WIN employers in fifteen different locations, the study examined the

process of this mutual adjustment. The most interesting aspect of the findings is that WIN workers once
successfully placed on a job are treated like, behave
like, and perform like the "regular" employees on the
same kinds of jobs. WIN employees seem to be a heter-
ogeneous group and frequently neither organization
managers nor supervisors know of these employees' WIN
background or training.

Another major finding of this study is that few of the
contextual features of WIN jobs--type of organization,
administrative policies, characteristics of the work
unit, or employer attitudes--had significant effects
on the successful integration of WIN employees into
the work force. However, WIN employees were found to
be more successful in small organizations in which
close, informal relationships and flexible atmosphere
prevail. This is perhaps related to another important
finding: former employees who left their WIN jobs
voluntarily, usually did not do so because of dis-
satisfaction with contextual factors, over which
employers have some control--such as administrative
conditions, formal rewards or status--but rather because they were dissatisfied with the job task itself;
had unsatisfactory interpersonal relations on the job;
had personal problems such as health or child care; or
wished to further their education and training.

The writers of the study point to an interesting para-
dox springing from their finding. The primary basis
for employer satisfaction with, and recruitment of,
employees is not job performance and skill levels but
employee attitudes, behavior, and personal appearance.
For the WIN employee, however, job satisfaction and
retention are based primarily on the nature of the job
task itself, so that skill training is of central
importance. This phenomenon, the writers conclude,
provides ambiguous direction as to which particular
component should be emphasized during the WIN experience. Perhaps the suggestion is that all aspects of
employment, from skill to good personal appearance,
should be addressed.

Training components did not seem significant in Schiller's study as well. With a population of 635 WIN
participants in 36 different sites, Schiller studied
the effectiveness of the program on the basis of four
criteria: job placement, employment preparation,
quality of job placement, and completion of the program. His overall conclusion is that WIN has a
positive influence upon some participants, as 76% of

those who stayed with the program were able to get and maintain jobs. While only 19% of the dropouts became employed, Schiller could not connect with certainty the impact of any of the program components.[9]

One of the frequently quoted studies is that of Ronald Fine undertaken for the Institute of Interdisciplinary Studies. Fine's study is an effort to describe the economic advantages and disadvantages to taxpayers and to clients of attempting to train and employ female-heads of AFDC families under varying social, demographic, and economic conditions.[10] Getting their population from select counties in three states-- Michigan, Minnesota, and Florida--Fine and his associates collected data over a two year period for a short term, cost-benefit analysis of the program. Their major conclusions are that: 1) the best predictors of employment and earning outcomes were existence of at least high school education, employment history, and earnings at intake; 2) the WIN program, with the possible exception of vocational training, has not resulted in increased employment and earnings; 3) WIN has not resulted in substantial financial pay-off to either clients or taxpayers. Fine's overall conclusion is that it is rather illogical to try to develop comprehensive referral guidelines for welfare mothers "to a group of services which are of no apparent value to them or to the taxpayers."[11]

The issue of making appropriate referrals has also been examined by the Wisconsin study conducted by the Institute for Research on Poverty. The study is based on a survey taken in 1967 exploring the recipients' work histories and attitudes toward work, their knowledge of the treatment of earned income and their experiences with the caseworkers on employment problems. The objective was to evaluate the WIN program's promise and potential. The aspects of this study which relate to the recipients' histories and attitudes gave similar findings as in the previously discussed studies. As for the recipient's experience with the welfare caseworkers, the study indicated that this experience will very much influence the recipient's experience with the WIN. The nature of the referral is, of course, at the basis of this relationship. The writers argue that whether the legislation requires these referrals to be voluntary or not, it is at the level of implementation that the nature of "voluntary" or "non-voluntary" takes shape. Their point is that "upon closer examination, another 'new direction' in welfare policy looks pretty much like the same old pattern. The administration of employment services for AFDC will: a) be highly decentralized and subject to broad administrative direction at the local level and b) touch very few AFDC recipients. In this respect, the rehabilitative services of WIN are no different from other social service programs that have been enacted for AFDC."[12] The authors conclude that "despite the changes in the laws and despite the political rhetoric, the issues of work and welfare will still be solved at the local level. The WIN program merely asks an existing welfare bureaucracy with an existing clientele to respond to a new program. For the vast majority of AFDC recipients, local welfare administration practices will be far more important than the WIN program."[13]

The importance of administration practices--the WIN's this time--was emphasized by another study whose main focus was the problem of WIN drop-outs.[14] Franklin undertook a longitudinal study in order to determine why enrollees terminate prematurely from their program. His major finding is that the "In-Out" status was significantly affected if the enrollee was assisted in preparing herself for entering the program, in working out employability plans, and in handling general difficulties that the training presented. From the perspective of the staff, Franklin found that drop-outs were viewed as those with presumed individual deficiencies, often plagued by serious problems, who entered WIN with low motivation (subsequently reflected in poor performance and relationships), had more unrealistic job objectives and rejected alternative suggestions. It was the staff's belief that both drop-outs and those who completed employability plans were subjected to essentially the same organizational processes. That is, the staff identified few organizational differences in the treatment provided to the two groups, and few procedures that needed changing. Franklin points to the importance of communication between the engaged members so that assessment of potentialities and expectations may be presented and dealt with efficiently.

Organizational variables were the focus also of the Dubey study.[15] More specifically, Dubey and his associates explored the social service decision-making process in order to determine the kind of manpower information, knowledge, and understanding needed for such a process to be effective. The approach was three-fold: through the welfare worker assigned to

the WIN team, the client, and the member of the WIN
team. Actually, the Dubey study is a part of a larger
project, undertaken by three universities, examining
the same issues in three different cities: Chicago,
Cleveland, and Detroit.[16]   And perhaps this is the
best contribution of this project, since the most
impressive finding is that there are significant differences among the three cities in the attitude and
perception of WIN workers in respect to the client and
the agency's goals. The general conclusion of the
researchers is that "the variation in the attitude and
perception of the team members appeared to be more a
function of the program in which the team members were
located rather than the team position they held."[17]
As for their findings regarding the welfare workers
and clients, these coincide with findings in other
studies already discussed in this review.

A more comprehensive appraisal of organizational issues surrounding WIN was undertaken by the Urban
Institute for the Employment and Training Administration of the Department of Labor.[18]   The research
was directed at identifying those organizational
characteristics that are systematically associated
with high WIN performance. Criteria measuring
performance were: 1) number of job entries per staff;
2) average job entry wage; 3) retention rate; and 4)
average monthly welfare grant reduction. The findings
made it clear that high performance is associated with
differences in the socio-economic environments over
which the administration and staff of the WIN have
little or no control. Labor market conditions--such
as the presence of low wage industries, and average
employer size--counted for a variation of 52.1% in the
performance of the program. Nevertheless, some organizational variables were found to have considerable
influence in the program's performance. High performing state WIN programs tended to be managed
differently than low performing ones. The leaders
imparted to local WIN sponsors and staff a clearer
perception of national program goals, including the
desirable quality and quantities of job entries. In-
ternally, they were able to provide clearer messages
to the staff as to expectations, allow more flexibility regarding work rules and office procedures,
delegate more program authority to subordinates, and
establish better accountability standards. As for the
clients, they seemed to be more the focus of attention
in the high performing WIN units than in those with
lower rates of success.

Comparative was the nature of the Klausner study as well.[19] He and his associates questioned a panel of husbandless AFDC recipients and a panel of husband-less, low-income working mothers. Klausner's effort was to evaluate what it takes to make such adults economically independent. The value of this study is based on its comprehensiveness rather than originality of its findings. There is nothing in this study that has not been already discussed in this review. Perhaps one interesting point is the researchers' consideration that manpower policy, when addressed to women, should be geared to their specific needs. The suggestion is that the concept of an economic incentive and labor force classifications are suited more to the motives and work career of a male rather than of a female labor force. As such, it is bound to impinge upon the program's (WIN) outcome.

The theme of social and attitudinal discrimination against[20] women workers is supported by Georgina Smith's study. Her emphasis, however, is on the lower paying status that women's jobs have in the market place. She attributes to this status the financial dependency of WIN graduates rather than to the nature of their training. In an effort to assess WIN's influence in moving welfare mothers to productive employment, Smith studied the WIN scene in two New Jersey cities where the labor market conditions seemed favorable. Her approach included comparisons between WIN enrollees and welfare mothers who did not enter the program; before and after views of the program by the enrollees; and characteristics of enrollees associated with successful employment, termination of training and prolonged training. She concludes that, given a favorable market and sufficient time, WIN appears capable of correcting the employment handicaps of most enrollees. Smith concedes that the training process takes a long time, but she argues that, regardless of the skill or training, most women cannot earn enough to support a family because[21] of existing sex discrimination in the labor market.

A number of follow-up studies seem to support Georgina Smith's findings that WIN did indeed improve the status of some women. Garvin and his associates, for instance, reviewing WIN participants nine months after they had entered WIN, found that, although only a few trainees had completed their employability plan, those who did obtained reasonably[22] good clerical, technical, and even professional jobs. In a more longitudinal study, Audrey Smith and her associates reached the

23

same conclusion. Their findings in the Chicago WIN program indicated that participants did move up the occupational ladder.[23] Wiseman, too, found that even those mothers who had worked before did significantly better after the WIN training.[24] These findings are confirmed by the research of Garfinkel[25] and of Auerbach Associates.[26] The latter, evaluating a national sample of WIN trainees from entry through a twelve-month period after leaving the program, determined that the financial gain is more substantial for women than men.

Overall, as Richardson[27] concludes, WIN apparently has helped certain persons gain skills that enable them to obtain and hold onto jobs, even though it is not possible to identify those skills or trace the positive effects to participants in specific WIN components. It must be noted, however, that the consensus among the above studies is that the overall number of people so positively affected by the WIN training is very small. The Auerbach Associates study, for instance, found that almost three out of four participants remained on AFDC throughout the year following termination.[28] Garvin, to use another example, places the successful rate at only nine percent of the enrollees.[29]

There is some controversy whether WIN II has been more successful in securing jobs for participants than WIN I. With an emphasis on job placement, WIN under the Talmadge amendments has indeed placed more persons in jobs than did WIN I.[30] But research has shown that placement rates as such are not the crucial issues.[31] "What is crucial is the extent to which WIN graduates obtain higher paying jobs and hold them longer than a comparable group that does not receive WIN services. The evidence in that respect suggests that WIN I was more effective than WIN II."[32] Also there are more WIN I trainees that are able to hold on to their jobs than WIN II graduates.[33] Schiller's 1974 panel study indicates that 83% of those who completed training under WIN I were still employed three years after their placement. Only 58% of WIN II were doing so. Perhaps it is even more interesting--though confusing in its implication--that 34% of WIN I drop-outs were employed three years after their premature termination of their training.[34] While Schiller's study is inconclusive as to the factors influencing these outcomes, it suggests that there were no clear employability plans in operation during the WIN II training.

What seems to be more conclusive is that taking part
in WIN has some beneficial effect on participants'
feelings about themselves and on their children. This
was Thompson and Miles' finding when they tried to
relate characteristics of participants to the outcome
of the program.[35] Working with 1200 black and white
women entering WIN at 30 different times in an eight
month period, these researchers were unable to pin-
point the reasons for success of the WIN program.
They did identify an improvement in self-respect on
the part of the participants. However, this effect
was found to be independent of whether the women were
able to obtain jobs or not.

Perhaps the most extensive attempt to evaluate the
impact of WIN was undertaken by Schiller and his associates.[36] Theirs was a longitudinal study, spreading
over a year and one half in time, and over 78 sites
across the country. Their population consisted of
2,500 WIN participants and more than 2,500 registrants
in the WIN pool but not yet participating in the program. Comparing their subjects' incomes before and
after training, the researchers found no significant
impact of the WIN effort on welfare costs. While
there were some participants, especially men, who were
able to remove themselves from the Public Assistance
rolls, overall WIN training did not seem sufficient to
resolve the welfare issue. More importantly, though,
the researchers found no significant relationship
between the kind and amount of services offered at the
sites and the subsequent earning of WIN participants
at those sites.

While the above studies emphasize the training and
educational opportunities of the WIN program as the
factors for the change in the status of the WIN enrollees, Schiller suggests that their job placement
depended almost entirely on the level and structure of
the demand for labor[37] and on community attitudes
towards WIN clients. Still others attribute all[38]
outcomes to the very nature of WIN policy. Appel,[38]
for instance, explores the governmental economics of
the policy.[39] So do Mildred Rein[40] and Ehrenberg and
Hewlett.[41] Smith and Ulysan,[42] as well as Burke and
Townsend,[42] concentrate on the financial incentives of
the recipient to enter the WIN program, which the
authors find minimal.[32] The other side of the coin is
viewed by Goldstein[32] who analyzes the disincentives
inherent in the policy. Such disincentives, Goldstein
concludes, are numerous and forceful and are to be

25

found both in the restrictions the program imposes--
such as reductions of in-kind benefits as earnings
increase--as well as in the indulgences it allows--
such as absence of penalties for non-compliance.
Given these disincentives, Goldstein points out, "it
is remarkable that WIN's placement rate is as high as
it is."[44] A somehow different argument is debated on
the one hand by Levitan, Rein and Marwick[45] who see
WIN succeeding only in conjunction with a more
comprehensive social welfare effort; and on the other
by Shatz and Steinberg[46] who simply consider WIN "a
pseudo-program," because of its lack of ideological,
financial, and political commitment to the goals it
posits.

Overall it can be said that research findings show, at
best, mixed results with respect to participants
gaining a secure place in the world of work. The
following discussion of the literature is aimed at
developing a more comprehensive understanding of the
reasons for such limited outcome.

WIN as a Policy of Social Welfare

One of the explicit aims of the WIN legislation has
been to assist welfare recipients to achieve "self-
support" or "personal independence" through employment.[47] This is not a minor task. There seems to be
the general consensus in the literature that all efforts to train welfare recipients to join the labor
force can be of no practical use unless there are
available jobs for them to fill; that the available
jobs should provide a substantially better living than
relief; and that the cost of the program should not
exceed the benefits it offers. In addition, WIN has
been charged with the thrust to contribute to this
country's economic growth through: a) saving public
funds via reduction of welfare loads, and b) increasing public revenues via the[48] productivity of
hitherto unutilized human resources.

Whether the above targets are containable within the
design of the WIN program is a seriously argued question. Heins, for instance, points out that programs
designed to increase employment are not necessarily
superior in a welfare sense to simple transfer programs, nor are they any more practical in terms of
cost-benefit analysis.[49] WIN has not proved to be an
exception. Findings show that the program has not

yielded enough cash gain to offset the cost of training.[50]   Actually, it is believed that investments in
human resources have not been efficient in raising
measured output as are alternative investments of a
more direct trade-off value.[51]   It has been even suggested that a given welfare increase can be achieved
at lower cost with head grants than with either a
negative income tax or a public employment program.[52]
That is, although a work subsidizing employment program may increase inducements for the poor to work, it
is not guaranteed that the resulting increase in value
of product would be as great as the value of the sub-
sidy required to generate its forthcoming. As Heins
puts it ". . . you might get the poor to work harder
by emphasizing employment subsidies rather than the
dole, but the fruits of that work may not justify the
cost to the rest of the society."[53]

The cost should not be evaluated only on the basis of
the traditional concern for the cost to the taxpayers.
After all, a welfare system, through its effects on
the incentives for work and family formation will, by
consequence, influence the behavior of a larger proportion of the population. As Durbin points out, any
work allowance or incentive program "increases the
critical cut-off point in the income distribution
below which people's work incentive and family patterns are affected by the welfare alternative."[54]   She
urges a careful evaluation of the impact of incentive
budget schemes on other poor people.   "Inasmuch as
such a program could provide incentives for particular
groups to come on welfare to benefit from the program,
it must be judged on its effects on those not on welfare earning less than the total income the incentive
scheme would allow."[55]   The Ehrenberg and Hewlett
study[56] indicates that this is one of the effects of
WIN.

Even if we ignore the question of inequity implied
here--the penalty to people for not applying for wel-
fare--the incentive system has the obvious effect of
making most individuals economically better off if
they are[57] in both the welfare system and the incentive
system.   Benefits in selected Public Assistance
categories have risen faster than wages. Moreover, in
some states benefit levels for those who participate
in training can be substantially higher than the wages
that can be secured from many jobs in the economy.[58]
When food stamps, health care, and perhaps public
housing benefits are added, and when child care and
other work-related expenses are considered, it is

27

apparent that jobs at or near the minimum wage are not a viable alternative to welfare for many recipients.

The dilemma of "less eligibility" is even more intricate if we consider the very nature of the WIN incentives. To quote Goldstein, "if the entire bureaucracy were to conspire against them, AFDC recipients could not be confronted with fewer[59] work incentives than the current system provides." On the other hand, Mildred Rein claims that the WIN incentive was given exceptional stature--and thus ascribed too great a potential--while in fact it was imbedded in an ongoing incentive system and therefore[60] bound to have very little effect on the work effort. Furthermore, ideological constraints in the WIN legislation and the practical problem of the cost of the program "led Congress to qualify in practice what it had espoused so vigorously in principle."[61] Modifications in the form of selectivity for enrollment, differentiation in training and sanctions for participation further mitigated the influence of the WIN incentives.

In order to avoid the dilemma of "less eligibility," it is suggested that we need policies which are not only directed at altering the capability and motivation of the supply of manpower[62] but which are directed as well at the supply system. As Durbin explains, "to the extent persons with no skills find it harder to find work, the possibility of receiving welfare income means welfare is in some sense compensating for the effect of the minimum wage." In other words, ". . . the provision of welfare income and the enforcement of minimum wage legislation operate together[63] and not separately to maintain the income floor."

What is suggested here, of course, is that full-time employment of the family head does not necessarily guarantee full-family support or economic self-sufficiency. A look at the OEO data[64] of the sixties will convince us of this argument. But even as specific a study as the Wisconsin one, undertaken by the Institute for Research on Poverty, has indicated that the WIN program can, if properly implemented, enhance the employability of recipients, but it cannot, "given their present productive powers and the amount of resources that will be invested in their rehabilitation, bring a large proportion of[65] them to total self-support within the near future." Findings support these predictions. Participation in WIN did not mean removal from welfare rolls for a large majority of people. As many as three out of four WIN trainees remained on AFDC throughout the year following termination.[66] So we move from welfare to supplementary welfare, so to speak, without substantially decreasing the welfare caseloads.

But then, as far as the welfare caseloads are concerned, even an increase of the minimum wage to subsistence level would not be of any critical value. There is sufficient evidence that such an increase always reduces the number of "low" jobs, thus increasing unemployment among the lowest skilled.[67] This is nothing less than full "recycling" of the welfare population, to use a very fashionable term.

It may be concluded, then, that the WIN program as a social welfare policy proves to be the symbol of the contradiction between the notion of using welfare for substitution and supplement, the "price stabilizers" as Rein calls it, and that of the "withering away" dream. As such, WIN is at its worst, a punitive, harsh measure for cheap labor, and at its best, an opportunity to give welfare mothers work experience to prepare themselves for the time when they leave welfare.[69]

Manpower Issues

As a manpower development program, WIN has drawn serious criticism. Bolino, for instance, accuses that ". . . the manpower-poverty budget continued based on rhetoric rather than reality . . . [its] commitments to reform [were] not matched by any determined effort to provide the money equal to the need."[70] Rein describes it as offering "a debate about policy choice in which there is little change; and . . . changes without explicit policy choices to support them."[71] And Gold concludes that "the lesson of WIN is not that a congressional program can fail, but rather that an antipoverty program founded upon the same faulty premises of previous unsuccessful schemes was doomed from the onset."[72]

What is obviously suggested here is that WIN, as designed, does not respond to the propositions of an adequate manpower program. Basic in such a program, according to the Committee for Economic Development, is the notion that training is "a phase in a larger system of continuing education" which provides opportunities for "vocational advancement . . . increased adaptability to take other jobs and cultural enrichment beyond the period of formal schooling."[73] Research in the job histories of WIN participants after their WIN experience has shown that the program has limited ability to provide such opportunities.[74] Goldstein, too, points out that after two years of operation only one percent of the assessed AFDC recipients had completed their training and been employed for a maximum of three months.[75] Others, as seen earlier, give a similar rate of success.[76] The percentage of those finding a permanent place in the world of work was even smaller.

If, on the other hand, unemployment is the frame of reference when establishing a manpower program, training can be considered as a way of making individuals employable and as "a means of keeping them maximally and optimally employed."[77] Such being the case, Borus and Tash present three sets of objectives to be met:

A. Those pertaining to government operations

1. Reduced cost of government operations
2. Reduced transfer payments
3. Increased tax revenues through increased tax base

B. Those pertaining to society

1. Improved equity in the distribution of income
2. Reduced unemployment
3. Increased GNP
4. Increased social satisfaction

C. Those pertaining to the individual

1. Increased income
2. Reduced unemployment
3. Increased social satisfaction.[78]

Some of the above points regarding the economic advantages of the WIN program have already been discussed in the previous parts of this chapter. It suffices here to restate that, although some studies suggest that vocationally-oriented training may show some promise for alleviating poverty,[79] it is neither an efficient nor an inexpensive way to raise the incomes of the poor. Sewell points out that "the productivity of workers should be measured in their hourly wage rates, and that increases in early levels associated

30

with training programs which are solely attributable to increases in the employment of trainees, may simply represent transfers of income from non-trainees to trainees."[80]

A cost-benefit evaluation of a manpower program must certainly include its opportunity cost and the value of the alternative benefits which are foregone because of the program.[81] It should also respond to the questions raised by Somers as to "whether the benefits to the trainees would be equally forthcoming in the absence of a government subsidized program," or "whether the jobs obtained by the trainees resulted primarily from the new skills acquired in their training or were other personal and labor market considerations more important."[82] This point is particularly valid in the case of the WIN program as research findings suggest that the ability to place enrollees depended almost entirely on the level and structure of the demand for labor rather than on variations in WIN training.[83] Goldstein agrees that WIN's ability to place trainees is very sensitive to cyclical economic conditions. He points out that "at current enrollment levels a one percentage point increase in the national unemployment rate increases the number awaiting job placement by an estimated 3,000 people. This is about equal to the number of trainees who successfully complete the program each month."[84] Even more interesting is Franklin's finding that a number of WIN dropouts obtained jobs as good or better than those of WIN graduates, perhaps because they were more skilled to begin with.[85]

Yet, cost-benefit analysis--in terms of economic efficiency--is only one of many ways by which a program's success can be judged. It does not give any final answers as to whether a program is good or justified, or whether it should be contracted or expanded.

Cain and Hollister suggest that, although increased rationality in the process of social planning is a very desired premise, the "rules of evidence" should not be limited to monetary considerations alone.[86] Barsby goes even further, stating that benefits that cannot be quantified are important enough to make it impractical to undertake a strict cost-benefit analysis. He proposes a "cost-effectiveness" model of decision making whenever nonmonetary measures enter into our calculations.[87] This seems to be particularly appropriate to the WIN program as a number of researchers argue. Their findings clearly indicate

that there are important nonmonetary dividends to WIN
trainees and their families.[88]

The issue made here is that manpower programs, like
many social programs, should not be simply responses
to the immediate economic and labor market needs. The
concept of investing in human resources is not a new
one. Economists have long ago widened their concept
of capital investment to include the capacity to create wealth along with the creation of wealth itself.[89]
Such investments, Sewell suggests, lead to "external
benefits for society as a whole, as well as those
private benefits which are captured by the individual."[90] Thus it is thought that one of the social
benefits of education is the creation of a more informed electorate.[91] Training programs for unemployed
youth have been promoted on the grounds that they may
reduce the social costs of juvenile delinquency.[92]
These are strong incentives to invest in the individual, yet they link programs which are important on
their own right with the solution of a problem with
which the public happens to be concerned. Thus, they
risk the danger that, if the outcome is not the specifically expected one--i.e., we still have juvenile
delinquency or welfare caseloads do not decrease--then
the program is discredited. Such a danger is very
realistic for the WIN program as the 1971 Social Security Amendments and recent changes in manpower
training policy indicate.

The development of human resources has more than one
implication, not the least being to help people "lead
fuller and richer lives, less bound by tradition."[93]
Observations from various studies indicate that vocational training graduates experience benefits other
than those measured by relative earnings.[94] Such
graduates, for instance, were able to pursue their
interest more closely, or had what Weisbrod calls an
"option value," that is access to "excess returns," to
opportunities for further pursuits and alternatives.[95]

To sum up this argument, as long as the objectives of
an employment-support program are limited to finding
jobs which are both unstable and low-paying, neither
is dependency going to be eradicated, nor personal
satisfaction to be attained.[96] With regards to the
WIN program, Mangum states that "although the base has
been established for a coherent program of remedial
services to the competitively disadvantaged . . .
there remain several limitations: the administrative

capability has yet to be developed for efficient delivery of services, and the resources committed are
grossly inadequate relative to need."[97]   He suggests
that solution to the first limitation would increase
the chances of solving the second. Sewell, on the
other hand, warns us that both goals--of economic
independence and personal satisfaction--involve great
cost in training programs for those disadvantaged to
the labor market, both because of the time element
involved in the training as well as because of "expenditures on items such as counseling services . . .
necessary to make this training effective."[98]

Work Ethic

Investments in human capital may also represent a
concession to a more austere principle. Stephen Marglin refers to it when he suggests that "the community
may not find it wholly satisfactory to achieve a given
redistribution of income by simply transferring cash
from one individual to another. . . . The size of the
economic pie and its division may not be the only
factors of concern to the community[99]the method of
slicing the pie may also be relevant."[99]

The current stance of welfare programs is, of course,
to encourage self-support. The challenge, we have
been told, is that "we are faced with a choice between
the work ethic that built this nation's character and
the new welfare ethic that causes the American character to weakness."[100]   There is an element of warning
in this concept of "workfare," one that suggests that
not only self-support is encouraged but that disin-
clination to achieve it is undesirable and, therefore,
punishable.

Rosenheim points out that although "the language of
repression and of penal goals has been discarded for
newer concepts phrased in terms of work incentive and
training or job skill upgrading,"[101] punitive over-
tones reminiscent of vagrancy law resound in present
welfare systems. Rosenheim, and TenBroek before her,
maintain that vagrancy concepts infuse the welfare
system and thus the family law of the poor. "Even
though their [vagrancy concepts] tenure in criminal
law appears to be in jeopardy . . . the relationship
of the poor law and other public aid provisions to the
vagrancy statutes is as intimate today as it was in
the time of the Tudors."[102]

The key element in vagrancy--as far as the individual welfare recipient is concerned--is, of course, the idea of idleness. Such an attack then on the welfare system may be seen as a disguised attack on the people the program is designed to serve. Friedman indicates that "fault" is a central concept in welfare law. He points out that the very work incentive is used very selectively. There have been no strong objections, for instance, to veterans benefits, yet such benefits have been quite high and of long duration. In his words: "no one can argue that high benefits will have a dangerous effect on incentive. But it seems quite easy to equate poverty with fault. American welfare legislation is scarred with the results of this atti-tude. It justifies setting benefit levels at a bare minimum. People must not be encouraged to get on the dole. . . . Actually, not much is known about the incentive problem. But belief in the incentive prob-lem is a political fact of central importance."[103]

There seems to be an inherent contradiction in such a belief. If the work ethic is such a basic value in American culture, why should it be lost in cases where subsistent living is secured? After all there are a tremendous number of financially independent people who work on a more than full-time basis. Is it true that "Horatio Alger is camp" as Morrison puts it? Is it true that welfare benefits reduce the absolute necessity of working or even make idleness less un-pleasant? Is it true that "not much remains of that proud heritage--the work ethic?" to quote Morrison again.[104]

Morrison himself answers that the work ethic is not lost in contemporary America. His own statistics indicate that more than 90% of all men in the country between the ages of 20 and 54 are either employed or actively seeking work. This is about the same percen-tage as twenty-five years ago. Over the past two decades the percentage of married women who work has risen from 25% to 42%. What is happening, Morrison says, is that the work ethic "is undergoing a radical transformation. Workers, particularly younger ones, are taking 'work' more seriously, not less. . . . [They] are willing to invest more efforts to their work, but are demanding a bigger payoff in satis-faction."[105] These findings were confirmed by the Special Task Force to the Secretary of Health, Educa-tion, and Welfare.[106] Their final report clearly indicates that the institution of work remains a cen-tral force in America. So pivotal is work in shaping

34

the quality of our lives, that satisfaction with work appears to be the best predictor of longevity, better than known medical or genetic factors.[107]

A study undertaken by the University of Michigan Survey Research Center attempted to rank various work aspects in order of importance for the worker. "Good pay" came in a distant fifth, behind "interesting work," "enough help and equipment to get the job done," "enough information to do the job" and "enough authority to do the job."[108] Another study, this one undertaken by Roessner, found that the most common reasons for leaving voluntarily were: the job task itself; unsatisfactory interpersonal relations at the job; personal problems, such as health, child care; or a wish to further training or education.[109]

It is evident from the literature that the work ethic is not meant as a senseless activity, but it reflects a much deeper value, the success ethic. Analysts of the American value system have emphasized the importance of the "success ethic," whether in the context of social mobility or in the meaning to the individual's identity.[110] It is the general consensus that the employment role is very important for an American. In their study, The Sociology of Retirement, Friedman and Havinghurst state that ". . . the job, or work activity can be regarded as an axis along which the worker's pattern of life is organized. It serves to maintain him in his group, to regulate his life-activity, to fix his position in his society, and to determine the pattern of his social participation and the nature of his life experience, and is a source of many of his satisfactions and affective experiences."[111] And, as Levitan and Johnson indicate, contemporary societies recognize that "the purpose of work includes not only what is to be accomplished but the human benefits and costs of accomplishing it."[112] They point to changes in governmental efforts to establish jobs. While in 1930's the emphasis was on creating employment and restoring the unemployed to their own line of work, in the 1960's the attention was shifted to opportunities for improving one's own social standing. Thus, "billions were spent to create entry-level, upward mobile jobs in health, education, community development and other fields which will benefit both employers and employees."[113] In the 1970's attention was turned to the needs of other groups of people, traditionally excluded from the labor market or having limited access to it. The new targets of employment policy became the disabled, women, the aged.[114]

There has been some evidence that leisure is our increasingly desired "good." But leisure is a very qualified commodity. Green, in his effort to examine how negative income taxation may influence incentives to work, points out that "if both income and leisure are 'normal' goods, and if preference patterns are not changed as a result of implementation of a negative income tax plan, utility maximizing individuals will choose to work less in the presence of tax payments than in their absence. How much less depends on the level of the income guarantee, the negative (marginal) cut rate and the share of the utility function."[115] What is implied here is that one's decision to work less will depend not so much on the attractiveness of the free time per se--leisure--but on the kind of life that the income will secure. This is no different than the concept of "substitution effect," that is, the phenomenon that increased income is associated with a decline in market work rates.[116] Green's analysis supports this point, indicating that "leisure might be reduced if leisure is an inferior good, if transfer payments by increasing recipient income changes 'life-styles' in such a way as to increase consumer unit's 'taste' for income relative to leisure, or if the assumption that the consumer unit makes no distinction between earnings and negative tax payments is relaxed."[117]

The modest and even gruesome standard of living permitted by the states could leave no argument as to the life-style available to welfare recipients. Moreover, Cain points out that the "substitution effect" does not hold exactly true for married women. His study indicates that over time the rise in income of families has been accompanied by a rise in work rates of wives.[118] Eyde suggests that a woman's eagerness to give up home work for employment does not stem from a reversal of the feminine mystique but rather from the following values: dominance-recognition value; interesting activity-variety value; and social value.[119] And, as far as the welfare population is concerned, there is no evidence to suggest the existence of a dichotomy between the work attitudes and aspirations of the working and non-working poor.[120]

The work ethic thus takes a different perspective. Roder suggests that "we should indeed work--not to 'earn our keep' by doing what machines can do much

36

better, but by developing to the fullest that which makes us different from these machines. . . . We must work at realizing our potentials as unique and creative beings instead of becoming mutilated replicas of the highest bidder's specifications."[121] This definitely coincides with the Aristotelian equation of work--[activity] with virtue but, again, meaningful activity; not activity as an end in itself, but as an accommodation to a feeling of purposeful life. Perhaps this perspective was best expressed by Douglas Frazer, the United Auto Workers' President, when he suggested that ". . . maybe we ought to stop talking about the work ethic and start talking about the life ethic."[122]

Characteristics of AFDC Recipients

No great research is needed to conclude that the AFDC program has never been widely popular. Nor has welfare for this matter. Miller, in one of his articles, gives many references from Gallup Poll releases to statements of judges and reporters, indicating that the popular stereotype of welfare recipients is one of a morally degenerate individual.[123] AFDC in particular has, over the years, been the "victim" of great underlying social changes which increased both its size as well as its makeup.

It has been the assumption that when AFDC was first established, husbandless mothers were considered outside the labor force and thus their children were among the "deserving poor." Handler and Hollingsworth suggest that this is a misleading view, and "whether or not dependent children were 'deserving' depended upon the social characteristics of their parents and the reason for the dependency."[124] Nevertheless, AFDC was based on the ethic that mothers of dependent children should not enter the labor force. Changes in attitudes toward working mothers have coincided with changes in the social characteristics of the AFDC population. So while the AFDC rolls increase in numbers, there seem to be more divorced, separated and unmarried mothers than widows, and increasingly more minority members, in them. Whatever the social, economic, and welfare policy factors for these changes, AFDC today, as Bernard puts it, "tends to serve a higher proportion of disadvantaged and disesteemed persons."[125] So we see a movement from the 1962 effort to encourage mothers to work, to the 1967 intent

37

to restore more families to employment, to the present
determination to establish the "workfare" ethic.

Yet, extensive research on the characteristics of AFDC
recipients and other poor have not substantiated the
popular notion of the "welfarized" person.   Carter,
for instance, reports that comparative data on the
welfare poor and other poor showed that, in general,
these two groups are the same--in terms of individual
and family characteristics.   "The found differences
lie in the immediate effect on marginal families of
external events that upset the last-straw, makeshift
provision for food and shelter."[126]   Goodwin's study
showed no difference in work orientation between AFDC
recipients and working women not on welfare.[127]   Similar were Garvin's findings.[128]   Prescott in his
investigation found no demographic differences between
AFDC-MDTA trainees and other AFDC recipients.[129]
Burnside maintains that AFDC women subscribe to the
work ethic regardless of their employment status.[130]
Her study of AFDC mothers in six states indicated that
these women emphasized the same advantages of working
as those discussed in the previous part of this
chapter.   Burnside found that "they [AFDC mothers]
believed that employment would bring independence and
pride to them and a better standard of living to their
families. . . They considered work a stimulus to
self-esteem."[131]   Bernard's study of mothers in the
Boston area who have been "high," "low," or "never"
users of welfare, showed that approximately the same
percentage from each group--and a high percentage at
that--would rather have a husband or employment than
be on welfare.[132]   And a study by Irene Cox of welfare
families in New York City indicated that seven out of
ten mothers said they would prefer to work rather than
stay home,[133] a percentage that corresponds to the
trend in the general population.   Perhaps more interesting, and more specific in its findings, is Opton's
study which, in evaluating a group of AFDC mothers
employed in California, suggested that many of the
conditions usually judged to be "barriers to employment," may not in fact be reasons for unemployment.
Opton concluded that "none of the following presumed
obstacles to employment--and typical targets of
welfare and labor programs--was related in a statistically significant degree to either unemployment or
to working more or working less: personality variables, motivation and attitudes about work and
welfare."[134]

Yet in their Michigan study, Smith and Ulysan found that, despite the significant increase in the employment rate which resulted from the 1967 Social Security Amendments' provision for exemption of earnings, the overall proportion of AFDC mothers who were employed remained at a relatively low level. They concluded that forces other than the degree of work incentive continue to constrain and influence the employment decision among AFDC mothers.[135]

What is then the difference between AFDC women and non-welfare poor mothers? Bernard's study suggested that "use of Public Assistance is related to one's place in the class structure. It is influenced by, and is part of, a network of connecting elements that form subcultural patterns. The elements, though forming an interlocking pattern, appear to be adjustments to the occupational system, with the key factors being the relative stability of the job, the skill required, and the pay received."[136]

What is implied here is that the employment potential of most of AFDC mothers can lead only to the lowest-paid, least-skilled, and highly-unstable occupations. For instance, in Burnside's study, service work was the most frequently reported occupation.[137] Opton, in his review of 1,000 recently closed AFDC cases in California, found no mothers who had become completely self-supporting through employment.[138] It is the general consensus that the main barrier to satisfactory employment is the very low educational level of welfare recipients. Although employed AFDC mothers are better educated than non-employed ones,[139] and although the total educational attainment of AFDC women had markedly improved during the recent years,[140] the educational level of both working and non-working AFDCers was found to be generally lower than for females 14 years old and over in the United States population, of whom 52% have completed high school.[141]

Not having a marketable skill, however, is not the sole reason for the unemployment of AFDC mothers. Eppley, in a study undertaken in 1969, found that less than one-half of the non-working AFDC mothers were so because of their inability to find stable employment. The rest were either incapacitated or, more often, were needed home.[142] Child care is, of course, an important issue for any working mother financially independent or not. However, for an AFDC mother, domestic responsibilities are even harder to dispense

39

with, not only because of her limited purchasing power
and generally restricted resources, but because of the
all-encompassing effects of these variables. What is
meant here is that day care centers may not be easily
accessible, transportation may not always be available, provided child care may not necessarily be
efficient, living conditions may not safeguard health,
and so on. Gans, for instance, reports in The Urban
Villagers that the incidence of problems was much
higher among the disadvantaged; professional services
and assistance were usually unavailable or too expen-
sive; and that trainees tended to have few financial,
political, and family resources to use in overcoming
the barriers.[143]

Thus, although a great number of studies substantiate
the proposition that training for skilled positions
increases the employability of AFDC women,[144] no manpower program can be successful or even adequate,
unless it takes into consideration the specific predicaments of these women.

Socio-Psychological Consequences of Poverty

What is suggested by the previous discussion is that
the welfare poor tend to be more impoverished and to
be afflicted by other problems to a greater extent
than non-welfare poor. Bernard found that non-users
of welfare have more resources of various forms available to them than welfare recipients.[145] Various
H.E.W. reports indicate serious nutritional hazards
resulting in vitamin deficiencies, anemic conditions
and other health problems. Langer and his associates
found a higher average ridit (average impairment risk)
among the members of welfare families.[146] And Hostetler talks about their exclusion from "the legal
process by which law is used, tested, challenged and
shaped to redress grievances and obtain justice."[147]
"Most important," Briar points out, "the welfare poor
live dependent on the operations of an institution,
the public welfare agency established to administer
welfare legislation."[148] What makes this last condition so important is that such institutions do not
inform the recipients of their rights and of the agency's obligation to them. Briar's study indicated that
"recipients think of themselves as supplicants rather
than rights-bearing citizens. And agencies reinforce
it.[149]

Prevalence of submissive attitudes toward authority among persons in low-income groups has been documented before.[150] But Briar's study is very cogent in its perception of the recipient's self-concept. Most of his respondents never referred to welfare recipients as "we" but as "they." Briar interprets, "this characteristic estrangement--also manifest in a tendency to view oneself as an atypical recipient, a self-conception which seemed to be held by nearly all the recipients interviewed--reflects the desire of these recipients to disassociate themselves from the image they have of other recipients. [Our] respondents expressed opinions about other public welfare recipients which usually have been associated primarily with conservative anti-welfare groups."[151]

Although Bernard indicated that "within this [his study's] population, stigma is not an important element in the determination to apply for assistance,"[152] there is enough evidence that the general concept of self-definition as bread-winner equals the self-definition as man.[153] Thus, "when we speak of poverty, we mean something more than material poverty and drain on the economy. The poverty we have in mind is as damaging to civilization as to the economy. . . . [I]t is the poverty of self-confidence [among the poor] and the image of themselves that slowly results from working below their capacity or not working at all."[154]

As stated earlier the employment role is very important to an American. Any aberration or insecurity in this role is apt to be reflected in a wide range of a person's activities, associations, and relationships. The psychological and social interconnection between working and non-working is most apparent when work is absent and long-time unemployment takes place. Simmons posits that if the world of work and the world of unemployment "were quite separate for the lower class worker, and he had no identification with work but only with money, then the unemployed long-time welfare recipient should show the same pattern of social relationships as is shown by the working person. The only disturbance manifested would result from the lowering of income level, and there should be no disturbance in the continuity of income created by intermittent employment. The fact of the matter is that studies of unemployment point to significant changes in the worker's self-definition and to development pattern of social withdrawal, which accompany his long-time unemployment."[155] Marienthal, a study done some time ago and recently republished,

41

indicated that prolonged unemployment leads to a state of apathy in which the victims do not utilize any longer even the few opportunities left to them.156 In his foreword to the new edition, Lazarsfeld, one of the original researchers, states that "the term 'breakdown of a social personality structure' is one way to tag the essential findings of <u>Marienthal</u>." He explains that the original German expression was "a reduction of the psychological life space," while his present choice of a term is "reduction of a man's effective scope."157 All very descriptive terms indeed.

The question then arises: Is there a vicious circle between economic deprivation, squashed hopes, lowered expectations, self-induced further reduction of effective opportunities? Aiken points out that there are at least two intellectual traditions which give official recognition to the existence of this circle.158 Both these traditions indicate that the political response to economic failure is political apathy, political alienation, sporadic bursts of extremist responses, and political radicalism. But such traditions seem to conceptualize anomie as mere lawlessness and thus may give rise to programs which merely "regulate the poor."

MacIver in his <u>The Ramparts We Guard</u> states that "anomy is a state of mind in which the individual's sense of social cohesion--the mainspring of his morale--is broken or fatally weakened. In this detachment of the anomic person from social obligation, his whole personality is injured.160 He has lost the dynamic unity of personality."160 When a person reaches such an "impoverished self-esteem,"161 when he loses the dignity and self-respect essential to his own work traditions and social standing, not only does he deteriorate as an individual, but the culture of which he is a part also tends to become a downgraded culture. Simmons states that "both the individual within his own cultural group, and the subculture within society as a whole are reduced to outcast status."162 It is here that the circle seems to become vicious. To quote Simmons again, we have here "the direct moral consequences of disturbing the motivational bases for socially meaningful work . . . without providing appropriate substitutes for the lost values."163

The issue is that a break through this circle cannot come unless we "reduce the social-emotional distance

42

between 'the keeper' and 'the kept.'"[164]   It is not
enough to open opportunities for people long deprived.
It is equally important to help them utilize their
chances. As Querry suggests, the effort is "to see a
person as a mixture of assets and liabilities. . . .
Much of the alleviation of the subtle effects of poverty and unemployment will come through specially
planned institutions set up to reeducate and revitalize the impoverished and unwanted."[165]

Delivery of Social Services

In a little article in the Journal of Public Social
Services, Spencer, who has helped organize a scholarship fund for welfare recipients in California, says
that "it is wiser to accept the premise that the process of building 'humanness' may well be as important,
if not more important, than the building itself."[166]
This is a useful perspective in evaluating service
delivery systems, especially in programs with such a
disputed design as in WIN. As Bateman puts it, "the
overall employment rate alone has little meaning for
evaluating program success. Aside from the obvious
narrowness of the measure itself, success must be
gauged by comparing what actually happened to participants as a result of training with what would have
happened if they had not enrolled."[167] In an attempt
to establish a way of identifying good and bad projects operating under similar constraints, Bateman
examined the training programs and work experience in
three different projects: One rural in eastern Ken-
tucky and two urban in Cleveland, Ohio, and St. Paul,
Minnesota. He found considerable variation in project
effectiveness, even after local labor market conditions and trainee characteristics were taken into
account.[168] He concluded that the process is indeed
fundamental to the outcome.

Aside from the purely technical aspects of a training
program, WIN's provision for supportive services is
the main "process." Ferman suggests that such services are designed to bring about "needed changes in
behavior" and to "ease the transition problem into the
world of work."[169]

If this mandate is to be understood in the terms pre-
scribed in previous parts of this chapter, that is, to
help the individual client construct a meaningful
life, then the essential strategy would be the design
of services that counteract or remove the barriers to

43

such a life. For instance, Briar suggests that, if a program is to make a person a "responsible citizen," it must be planned and operated in such a way that "it at least does not generate or reinforce attitudes of submissiveness and suppliance on the part of the recipients."[170]

There has been extensive literature on the nature of therapeutic interaction, too extensive, and too well known to need to be reviewed. Suffice here to remind us that in a helping relationship three aspects are of particular significance: the communication between the people involved, their attitudes, and their individual responses as expressed in their behavior.[171] Thus a concept like "hard to reach" implies something about the helper as well as the person considered in need of help. As Collins explains, "as members of the majority of the population, in our roles as practitioners, using the avenues of communication, the skills and techniques we know, we have not succeeded in achieving significant contact with them [the hard to reach]."[172] The same is valid for those needing employment. For "in the last analysis . . . it is a human being who declares another to be hard-to-employ or hard-to-place."[173] To transfer it to the WIN experience, what is important is not only the component the enrollee is in, but also more importantly, the exchange she has with the people helping her during her time in the component.

Collins is not the only one, of course, who emphasizes that in treatment one should consider one's behavior in the light of one's previous experience.[174] Yet an important point frequently overlooked is that the client's reactions to treatment may be affected "by factors outside the awareness of workers and ones over which they have little control."[175] Mayer and Timms, for instance, found that "clients who questioned the discretion of friends were buoyed up by the confidentiality of the casework situation. Conversely, those who received supportive--but not instrumental--help from their network were relatively unmoved by the bolstering efforts of their workers."[176] The authors rightly conclude that "an individual's interactions with friends and relatives--in addition to affecting the likelihood of his seeking professional help--will condition his later responses to treatment."[177]

The same authors point to another barrier to treatment effectiveness. "Professionals--whether doctors, lawyers, or social workers--tend to have certain notions

44

concerning the ways in which professional-client relationships should be structured. But clients are not
always aware of them,[178] or if they are, they do not
always accept them." Vinter elaborates on the
source of this phenomenon. He suggests that "treatment technologies can be considered in large part as
action correlates of . . . prevailing belief systems
[i.e., what constitutes deviancy, how it comes about,
and so on]. Thus the classification and diagnostic
systems utilized in treatment agencies have their
origins in such beliefs and, in turn,[179] they categorize
clients for organizational effort." As a result,
"change in a client is assessed more in terms of his
responses to the agency expectations and his relations
with other personnel than in terms of his capability
for conventional social role behavior. Such organiza-
tionally valued changes may not be merely irrelevant
to community performance requirements but, in extreme
form, may result in a client's trained incapacity[180] to
function adequately outside the agency."

The issue, therefore, is the kind of treatment technology which will be geared to the client's context,
on a particularistic rather than universalistic orientation, with emphasis on client individualization
rather than client categorization, to use two other of
Vinter's terms. The implication in such a goal-set-
ting is for a continuous innovation in method.
Actually, quite a host of new treatment modalities
have appeared, due in large part to renewed efforts to
reach the poor and, perhaps the emergence of community
mental health. As Mayer and Timms state, "the bur-
geoning of new practitioners has presumably terminated
the search for the 'one' most effective way of helping
troubled people."[181] In this sense "the concept of
hard-to-employ or hard-to-place is optimistic and
policy oriented. In particular it opens the possibility of gainful work for groups who previously have
been neglected entirely or aided chiefly through financial assistance."[182]

Organizational Issues

The previous discussion leads to an intellectual dilemma. If a program's goals are stated with reference
only to one party--whether the trainees, the government or the agency staff--effects on other parties,
both favorable and unfavorable effects, tend to be
neglected. This neglect may result in a spurious

assessment of the program in a sort of variation of the Hawthorne effect.

An organization, Max Weber tells us,[183] should be conceived as an "instrument," as a rational means to the realization of expressly announced group goals. "Its structures are understood as tools deliberately established for the efficient realization of these group purposes. Organizational behavior is thus viewed as consciously and rationally administered, and changes in organizational patterns are viewed as planned devices to improve the level of efficiency."[184] In such a concept of organizational format exchanges and interactions are essential as is "the dominance of a spirit of formalistic impersonality, without hatred or passion, and hence without affection or enthusiasm. The dominant norms are concepts of straight forward duty without regard to personal considerations."[185] But this is a "pure" type of bureaucracy--monocratic bureaucracy as Weber himself calls it--an ideal type which, as Albrow indicated, reveals a commitment to an objective social science. Albrow, in an excellent discourse on the multiconceptual aspects of bureaucracy, criticized Weber for his lack of concern for the problems of bureaucratic inefficiency. He says that "it is [bureaucracy's] very rationality which raises problems for democracy."[186] He explains that he finds this neutral concept of bureaucracy ademocratic in the sense that it ignores the existence of a variety of agents involved and thus it fails to take into consideration the influence of, and effects upon, these agents on each level of a policy's execution. Rosenheim refers to a similar concept in his example: If the policy adopted toward treatment of the able-bodied is characterized by suspicion and denial, it stands that it takes a toll from those executing the letter and the spirit of the law at the same time that

> it encourages slyness and chicanery by persons on the receiving end. . . . Harsh measures carry within them the seeds of corruption. At least within the Public Assistance program, workers sooner or later become committed to unbending application of rules or to most strenuous efforts to avoid intolerable severe consequences. Neither extreme promotes a reasonable consistency in administration nor creates an atmosphere in which legislative and administrative change is freely sought whenever conditions call for it.[187]

Parsons, on the other hand, views organization as a system, a "natural whole."[188] In such a model the realization of the stated goals is but one of several important needs to which the organization is oriented. Gouldner explains that such an organization "strives to survive and maintain its equilibrium, and this striving may persist even after its explicitly held goals have been successfully attained. Thus strain for survival may even on occasion lead to the neglect or distortion of the organization's goals."[189] Such organizations become very often ends in themselves and their preoccupation with maintenance may generate new objectives which definitely limit the manner in which the original goals can be pursued. Inherent in such development is the danger of confusion of purpose and absence of priorities to guide the expenditures of money and talent. To bring back Rosenheim's example of Public Assistance, to insist on a restrictive vision of the functions of welfare is to encourage a continuous redefinition of the problem without a balanced appraisal of policy. Blau found that this situational context of Public Assistance produces a "reality shock" which tends to create a distrustful and uninterested orientation toward recipients.[190] Perhaps the latter-day argument could be Specht's thesis of the security that social services represent--as versus the risks of new methodologies[191]--a very quick answer indeed to the old cause-function argument.

Blau and Scott classify formal organizations on the basis of their function rather than style. They suggest four types, one of which is "Service Organization" which is governed by the interests of the client.[192] The mandate in such organizations is that the client will remain always the focus of any organizational activity. Thus the structure, treatment methodology, even physical set-up, will depend on the client's needs. It is the implied understanding that the organization will cease to exist when these needs are met.

Actually Albrow indicates that there is "a bevy of competing concepts" of organizational structure,[193] and the literature overflows with paradigms and models of administration and management.[194] The issue is that in an organization much of the quality and structure of services will depend on what orientation the members of the organization subscribe to.[195] This is possible because actual bureaucracies are compounded by non-bureaucratic elements as well.[196] Important among these elements is the role the organization members are engaged into. Merton's concept of role set calls attention to the complement of role relationships which persons have by virtue of occupying a certain status.[197]   Thus the status of a worker in an agency involves individuals in role relationships with superiors in the organization, with clients, and with co-workers.   Each of these relationships has some bearing upon the way they perform their role as workers of the agency.   Thomas suggests that the ideal interaction encounter, from the perspective of role theory, is the "valid role synchrony,"[198] an exchange in which all parties involved know their purposes, their needs, and their capacities, and which is based on clear perception of each other's goals.

It is safe, therefore, to conclude that in a service delivery organization, where the operations are defined by the needs of the clients rather than by a "consistent system of abstract rules," valid role synchrony is facilitated. The resulting assumption is that in such organizational conditions there will be more flexibility in the nature of services offered, more freedom in the exchanges between the persons involved, more innovation in the approaches attempted, and more personal investment in the efforts made.

FOOTNOTES

CHAPTER II

1.   U.S. Department of Labor, Manpower Report of the President, Washington, D.C.:   U.S. Government Printing Office, 1974), p. 126.

2.   L. Goodwin, Do the Poor Want to Work? (Washington, D.C.: The Brookings Institution, 1972), p. 8.

3.   Ibid., pp. 10-12.

4.   Ibid., p. 51.

5.   Ibid., p. 102.

6.   D. Roessner, Employment Context   and Disadvantaged   Workers (Washington, D.C.:   Bureau of Social Science Research, Inc., 1971).

7. Ibid., p. 4.

8. Ibid., p. 192.

9. B. R. Schiller, The Impact of Urban WIN Programs (Washington: Pacific Training and Techical Assistance Corporation, 1972).

10. R. Fine, et al., Final Report: AFDC Employment and Referral Guidelines (Minneapolis: Institute for Interdisciplinary Studies, Welfare Policy Division, 1972).

11. Ibid., p. 29.

12. J. Handler and E. J. Hollingsworth, Work and the Aid to Families with Dependent Children (Madison: The University of Wisconsin, 1969).

13. Ibid.

14. D. Franklin, A Longitudinal Study of WIN Drop-Outs: Program and Policy Implications (Los Angeles: Regional Research Institute in Social Welfare, University of Southern California, 1972).

15. S. Dubey, et al., The WIN Research Project: Preliminary Program (Cleveland: School of Applied Social Sciences, Case Western Reserve University, 1970).

16. W. Reid, ed., Decision-Making in the Work Incentive Program (Chicago: School of Social Services Administration, University of Chicago, 1972).

17. Ibid., p. 212.

18. U.S. Department of Labor, Implementing Welfare-Employment Programs: An Institutional Analysis of the Work Incentive (WIN) Program, (R&D Monograph 78, Department of Labor, Employment and Training Administration, 1980).

19. S. Klausner, The Work Incentive Program: Making Adults Economically Independent (Philadelphia: Center for Research on the Acts of Man, 1972).

20. G. Smith, <u>Impact of Remedial and Supportive Services Upon Disadvantaged Job Applicants</u> (Rutgers: The State University of New Jersey, 1971).

21. Ibid., p. 26.

22. C. D. Garvin, <u>Incentives and Disincentives to Participation in the Work Incentive Program</u> (Ann Arbor: The University of Michigan School of Social Work, 1974).

23. A. D. Smith, et al., "WIN, Work and Welfare," <u>Social Service Review</u> 49:3 (September 1975), 396-404.

24. M. Wiseman, <u>Change and Turnover in a Welfare Population</u> (Berkeley: University of California, Department of Economics, 1976).

25. I. Garfinkel, "Income Transfer Programs and Work Effort: A Review," in <u>How Income Supplements Can Affect Work Behavior</u>, pp. 1-32, Studies in Public Welfare, paper No. 13 (Washington, D.C.: U.S. Government Printing Office, 1974).

26. <u>An Impact Evaluation of the Work Incentive Program</u> (Philadelphia: Auerbach Associates, 1972).

27. A. Richardson, <u>Youth in the WIN Program: Report on a Survey of Client Backgrounds, Program Experience and Subsequent Labor Force Participation</u> (Washington, D.C.: Bureau of Social Science Research, 1975).

28. Auerbach Associates, op. cit.

29. Garvin, op. cit.

30. U.S. Department of Labor, <u>The Work Incentive (WIN) Program and Related Experience</u> (R&D Monograph 49, U.S. Department of Labor, Employment and Training Administration, 1977).

31. B. R. Schiller, et al., <u>The Impact of WIN II: A Longitudinal Evaluation</u> (Washington: Pacific Consultants, 1976).

32. <u>The Work Incentive (WIN) Program and Related Experience</u>, op cit., p. 35.

33. E. Hokenson, et al., Incentives and Disincentives in the Work Incentive Program (Minneapolis: Interstudy, 1976).

34. B. R. Schiller, The Pay-Off to Job Search: The Experience of WIN Trainees (Washington: Pacific Training and Technical Assistance, 1974).

35. D. L. Thompson and G. H. Miles, The Characteristics of AFDC Populations That Affect Their Success in WIN (Minneapolis: North Star Research and Development Institute, 1972).

36. B. R. Schiller, et al., op. cit. (For a more comprehensive analysis of this study see The Work Incentive (WIN) Program and Related Experience, op cit., pp. 17-18).

37. B. R. Schiller (1972), op. cit.

38. G. L. Appel, Effects of a Financial Incentive on AFDC Employment: Michigan's Experience Between July 1969 and July 1970 (Minneapolis: Institute for Interdisciplinary Studies, 1972).

39. M. Rein, Work or Welfare? Factors in the Choice of AFDC Mothers (New York: Praeger Publishers, 1972).

40. R. B. Ehrenberg and F. G. Hewlett, The Impact of the WIN II Program on Welfare Costs and Recipient Rates, Technical Analysis, paper no. 15-C (Washington, D.C.: U.S. Government of Labor, 1975) (draft).

41. V. Smith and S. Ulysan, The Employment of AFDC Recipients in Michigan, Studies in Welfare Policy, Michigan Department of Social Services (June 1972) (mimeographed).

42. U. Burke and A. A. Townsend, Public Welfare and Work Incentives: Theory and Practice, Studies in Public Welfare, paper no. 14 (Washington, D.C.: U.S. Government Printing Office, 1974).

43. J. H. Goldstein, The Effectiveness of Manpower Training Programs: A Review of Research on the Impact on the Poor, Studies in Public Welfare,

51

paper No. 3 (Washington, D.C.: U.S. Government Printing Office, 1972).

44. Ibid., p. 8.

45. S. A. Levitan, M. Rein, and D. Marwick, Work and Welfare Go Together (Baltimore: The John Hopkins University Press, 1972).

46. E. Shatz and S. Steinberg, The WIN Program--An Appraisal (paper presented at the 98th Annual Forum, National Conference on Social Welfare, May 17, 1971, at Dallas, Texas; mimeographed copy).

47. 1967 Amendments to the Social Security Act, Title IV, Part C.

48. See, for instance, Michael Borus and William Tash, Measuring the Impact of Manpower Programs (Ann Arbor: Institute of Labor and Industrial Relations Publications, 1970), p. 14; E. Ginsberg and H. Smith, Lessons from Ethiopia (New York: Columbia University Press, 1967), pp. 33-44; S. Levitan and G. Mangum, Federal Training and Work Programs in the Sixties (Ann Arbor: Institute of Labor and Industrial Relations Publications, 1969), p. 274.

49. J. Heins, "The Negative Income Tax, Head Grants, and Public Employment Program: A Welfare Analysis," The Journal of Human Resources, Vol. 5, No. 3 (Summer, 1970), pp. 298-303.

50. Auerbach Associates, op. cit., J. Goldstein, op. cit., G. Smith, op. cit., see also Manpower Report of the President, 1974, op. cit.

51. B. Weisbrod, "Investing in Human Capital," Journal of Human Resources, Vol. 4, No. 1 (Summer, 1966), pp. 5-21; or "Education and Investment in Human Capital," Journal of Political Economy, Vol. 70, No. 1 (Supplement, October 1962), pp. 106-123.

52. For excellent discussions on this subject see: Heins, op. cit.; D. O. Sewell, Training the Poor: A Cost Benefit Analysis of Manpower Programs in the U.S. Anti-Poverty Program (Kingston, Ontario: Industrial Relations Centre,

Queens University, 1971); M. Rein, <u>Social Policy: Issues of Choice and Change</u> (New York: Random House, 1970), pp. 305-325; L. Greene, <u>Free Enterprise Without Poverty</u> (New York: W. W. Norton and Company, Inc., 1981).

53. Heins, op. cit., p. 303.

54. E. Durbin, <u>Welfare Income and Employment</u> (New York: Frederick A. Praeger, 1969), p. 141.

55. Ibid., p. 153.

56. Ehrenberg and Hewlett, op. cit.

57. Rein, op. cit., B. Berstein, "Welfare in New York City," <u>City Almanac</u> 4, No. 5 (February 1970).

58. Goldstein, op. cit.; Levitan, Rein and Marwick, op. cit., pp. 110-138; Rein, op. cit., pp. 317-322.

59. Goldstein, op. cit., p. 50. For more on this argument see Burke and Townsend, op. cit., p. 30.

60. M. Rein, op. cit., pp. 64-79.

61. Ibid., p. 85.

62. Durbin, op. cit., p. 21.

63. Ibid.

64. See the various articles by M. Orshanksy in the <u>Social Security Bulletin</u>, as for instance: "Counting the Poor: Another Look at the Poverty Profile," 28:1 (January 1965), p. 29; "Who's Who Among the Poor: A Demographic View of Poverty," 28:7 (July, 1965), pp. 3-32; "Recounting the Poor--A Five Year Review," 29:4 (April, 1966), pp. 20-37.

65. L. Hausman, "The Welfare System as Rehabilitation and Manpower System," quoted in Handler and Hollingsworth, <u>Work, Welfare and the Nixon Reform Program,</u> Reprint 60 of the Institute for Research on Poverty (May, 1970), p. 937.

66. For a comprehensive review see <u>Manpower Report of the President</u>, op. cit., 1974. See also <u>The Work Incentive (WIN) Program and Related Experience</u>.

67. Durbin, op. cit., pp. 13-24; Rein, op. cit., p. 320.

68. Rein, op. cit., p. 308. See also Durbin's comment that "as welfare is increasingly used--not just as support, but to provide a socially acceptable minimum for all--welfare becomes more a <u>supplement</u> to labor market earning from society's point of view" (emphasis hers), pp. 21-22; or Sidney Bernard, <u>The Economic and Social Adjustment of Low Income Female-Headed Families</u>, unpublished dissertation (Brandeis University, 1964). He states that "differential use of public assistance can be interpreted as a utilitarian form of adjustment to unstable participation in the occupational structure," p. 17.

69. Handler and Hollingsworth, op. cit., p. 937.

70. A. Bolino, <u>Manpower and the City</u> (Cambridge, Mass.: Schenkman Publishing Company, 1969), p. 257.

71. Rein, op. cit., p. 323.

72. Gold, as cited in Reid and Smith, op. cit., p. 485.

73. Committee for Economic Development, <u>Training and Jobs for the Urban Poor: A Statement of Policy</u> (New York: 1970), p. 43.

74. <u>Manpower Report of the President</u>, op. cit., 1974. Also, <u>The Work Incentive (WIN) Program and Related Experience</u>, op. cit.

75. Goldstein, op. cit., p. 52.

76. See, for instance, <u>The Work Incentive (WIN) Program and Related Experience</u>.

77. I. Hoos, <u>Retraining the Work Force</u> (Berkeley: University of California Press, 1967), p. 264.

78. M. Borus and W. Tash, op. cit., pp. 10-14.

79. T. Ribich, Education and Poverty (Washington, D.C.: The Brookings Institution, 1968), pp. 97-98; E. Stromsdorfer, "Determinants of Economic Success in Retraining the Unemployed. The West Virginia Experience." The Journal of Human Resources, 3:2 (Fall, 1968), 139-158; Sewell, op. cit., p. 4.

80. Sewell, op. cit., pp. 108-109. Sewell argues that these "allocative distributional effects" may even be regressive in their impact on the distribution of income. See also Durbin, op. cit., and Heins, op. cit.

81. S. Barsby, Cost-Benefit Analysis and Manpower Programs (Lexington, Mass.: Lexington Books, D. C. Heath and Company, 1972), p. 15. Barsby even suggests that the assessment should include the program's "vacuum effect," that is, the number of jobs vacated by the participants that were filled by workers who would otherwise have been unemployed.

82. G. Somers (ed.), Retraining the Unemployed (Madison: University of Wisconsin Press, 1968), pp. 149-167.

83. Manpower Report of the President, op. cit., 1974. See also The Work Incentive (WIN) Program and Related Experiences.

84. Goldstein, op. cit., p. 7.

85. Franklin, op. cit.

86. G. Cain and R. Hollister, "Evaluating Manpower Programs for the Disadvantaged," in G. G. Somers and W. D. Wood (eds.), Cost-Benefit Analysis of Manpower Policies (Ontario: Industrial Relations Centre, Queen's University of Kingston, 1969), pp. 149-150.

87. Barsby, op. cit., pp. 11-13.

88. See, for instance, G. Smith, op. cit.; Schiller, 1972, op. cit.; Richardson, op. cit.; Thompson and Miles, op. cit.

89. G. Myrdal, _Asian Drama_ (New York: Pantheon, 1968), p. 1543.

90. Sewell, op. cit., p. 2.

91. A. Marshall, _Principles of Economics_ (London: Macmillan, 1966), as quoted in Sewell, op. cit., p. 2.

92. See for instance Richard Cloward and Lloyd Ohlin, _Delinquency and Opportunity_ (New York: The Free Press, 1960).

93. Sewell, op. cit., p. 2.

94. Barsby, op. cit., pp. 32-35.

95. Weisbrod, op. cit.; Sewell, op. cit.

96. G. Carter, "The Employment Potential of AFDC Mothers," _Welfare in Review_, 6:4 (July-August, 1968); Sewell, op. cit., p. 3.

97. G. Mangum, "Evaluating Manpower Programs," in _Manpower Problems and Policies_, John Delehanty (ed.), (Scranton, Pa.: International Textbook Company, 1969), pp. 353-363.

98. Sewell, op. cit., p. 110.

99. S. Marglin, "Objectives of Water-Resource Development: A General Statement" in Arthur Maas, et al. (eds.), _Design of Water Resource Systems_, as quoted in Sewell, op. cit., p. 3.

100. D. Morrison, "Is the Work Ethic Going Out of Style?" Quoting from President Nixon, _Time_ (October 30, 1972), p. 96.

101. M. Rosenheim, "Vagrancy Concepts in Welfare Law," in J. TenBroek (ed.), _Law of the Poor_ (San Francisco: Chandler Publishing Company, 1966), p. 206.

102. Ibid., p. 187. For an excellent discussion of this issue, see also J. TenBroek, "California's Dual System of Family Law: Its Origin, Development and Present Status," _Stanford Law Review_, Vol. 16 (March 1964), pp. 257-317 (July 1964), 900-981; and Vol. 17 (April 1965), pp. 614-632.

103. L. Friedman, "Social Welfare Legislation: An Introduction," _Stanford Law Review_, Vol. 21 (January, 1969), pp. 223-224.

104. Morrison, op. cit., p. 96.

105. Ibid., p. 97.

106. _Work in America_, op. cit.

107. Ibid., pp. 76-92.

108. Quoted in Morrison, op cit., p. 97.

109. D. J. Roessner, _Employment Context and Disadvantaged Workers_ (Washington, D.C.: Bureau of Social Science Research, 1971), p. 192.

110. See for instance Horney's notion of anxiety--the competitive struggle for survival, the notion that if you don't trust people you want to be ahead of them or better than they; or see Sorokin's ideas of social stratification, etc.

111. E. Friedman and R. Havinghurst, _The sociology of Retirement_, as quoted in Michael Aiken, et al., _Economic Failure, Alienation and Extremism_ (Ann Arbor: The University of Michigan Press, 1968), p. 2. See also M. Jahoda, et al., _Marienthal-- The Sociography of an Unemployed Community_ (New York: Aldine-Atherton, Inc., 1971).

112. S. A. Levitan and W. B. Johnson, _Work is Here to Stay, Alas_ (Salt Lake City: Olympus Publishing Company, 1973), p. 173.

113. Ibid.

114. See, for instance, S. A. Levitan and R. Taggart, _Jobs for the Disabled_ (Baltimore: The John Hopkins University Press, 1977).

115. C. Green, "Negative Taxes and Monetary Incentives to Work: The Static Theory," _The Journal of Human Resources_ (Summer, 1968), p. 280.

116. G. Cain, _Married Women in the Labor Force: An Economic Analysis_ (Chicago: University of Chicago Press, 1966), p. 7.

117. Green, op. cit., p. 288.

118. Cain, op. cit., pp. 1-4. It is interesting to note that the most rapid increase in work rates of wives has come since 1940, during a period when birth rates have risen sharply. That is, the cross-section relationship between the presence of children and work rates is consistently negative. Of course, during the same time the public's attitudes toward women in employment have been increasingly more receptive which is another indication of the cultural influence of taste and, therefore, its changeability.

119. L. Eyde, Work Values and Background Factors as Predictors of Women's Desire to Work (Research Monograph No. 108, Bureau of Business Research, (Columbus: The Ohio State University, 1962), p. 20.

120. Garvin, op. cit., Goodwin, op. cit.

121. F. Roder, "Why Work?" The Journal of Public Services (March, 1971), p. 4. See also Maslow's concept of self-actualization.

122. Quoted in Morrison, op. cit., p. 97.

123. H. Miller, "Characteristics of AFDC Families," Social Service Review, 39:4 (December 1965), pp. 399-409.

124. Handler and Hollingsworth, op. cit., p. 908.

125. S. Bernard, The Economic and Social Adjustment of Low-Income Female-Headed Families (unpublished dissertation, May, 1964), p. 7.

126. Carter, op. cit., pp. 1-11.

127. Goodwin, op. cit.

128. Garvin, op. cit.

129. E. Prescott, et al., "Training and Employability: The Effects of MDTA on AFDC Recipients," Welfare in Review (January-February, 1971), pp. 1-6.

130. B. Burnside, "The Employment Potential of AFDC Mothers in Six States," Welfare in Review (July-August, 1971), pp. 16-20.

131. Ibid., p. 19.

132. Bernard, op. cit., pp. 79-83.

133. I. Cox, "The Employment of Mothers as a Means of Family Support," Welfare in Review (November-December, 1970), p. 26.

134. E. Opton, Factors Associated with Employment Among Welfare Mothers, in R. Fine, AFDC Employment and Referral Guidelines: Final Report, report to the Department of Health, Education and Welfare (June, 1972), p. 259.

135. Smith and Ulysan, op. cit.

136. Bernard, op. cit., pp. 153-154.

137. Burnside, op. cit., p. 16.

138. Opton, in Fine, op. cit., p. 259.

139. Burnside, op. cit., p. 17.

140. P. Levinson, "How Employable are AFDC Women?" Welfare in Review (July-August, 1970), p. 16.

141. As this is shown in the 1969 Bureau of the Census, U.S. Department of Commerce--Population Characteristics Report No. 194, Series P-20, February, 1970. Reported in Burnside, op. cit., p. 17.

142. D. Eppley, "The AFDC Family in the 1960's," Welfare in Review (September-October, 1970), p. 14.

143. H. Gans, The Urban Villagers (Glencoe, Ill.: The Free Press, 1962).

144. See Carter, Burnside, Prescott, Bernard, op. cit., etc.

145. Bernard, op. cit., p. 39.

146. T. Langer, et al., "Psychiatric Impairment in Welfare and Non-Welfare Children," Welfare in Review (March-April, 1969).

147. Z. Hostetler, "Poverty and the Law," in Poverty as a Public Issue, B. Seligman (ed.), (New York: The Free Press, 1965), pp. 177-178.

148. S. Briar, "Welfare from Below: Recipients' Views of the Public Welfare System," in Ten-Broek, The Law of the Poor, op. cit., p. 47.

149. Ibid., p. 59.

150. See for instance the discussion in Berelson and Steiner, Human Behavior: An Inventory of Scientific Findings, in Briar, ibid.

151. Briar, op. cit., p. 51.

152. Bernard, op. cit., p. 168.

153. See Part D1 of this chapter.

154. W. Querry, Illness, Work and Poverty (San Francisco: Jossey-Bass, Inc., 1968), p. 6.

155. H. Simmons, Work Relief to Rehabilitation (Sacramento: The Citadel Press, Inc., 1969), p. 14. See also the studies of E. Wight Bakka, The Unemployed Man (London: Nisbet and Co., Ltd., 1933) or Citizens Without Work (Haven: Archon Books Edition, 1969); Herbert Gans, The Urban Villagers, op. cit.; Karl Polanyi, The Great Transformation (New York: Beacon Press, 1944).

156. Jahoda, et al., op. cit.

157. Ibid., p. X.

158. Aiken, et al., op. cit., The two traditions: "The Mass Society Hypothesis" and "The economic Insecurity Hypothesis," p. 199.

159. See for instance F. Piven and R. Cloward, Regulating the Poor (New York: Pantheon Books, 1971); also James Dumpson, "The Commitment," Part I of: "Public Welfare--Recommitted, Restructured, Revitalized," in M. Morton (ed.), Can Welfare Keep Pace? (New York: Columbia University Press, 1969), pp. 44-61.

160. R. M. MacIver, The Ramparts We Guard (New York: Macmillan, 1950), p. 85.

161. Querry, op. cit., p. 9.

162. Simmons, op. cit., p. 9.

163. Ibid.

164. Querry, op. cit., p. 11.

165. Ibid., p. 9.

166. M. Spencer and J. Stephen, "An Alternative to Do-Nothingness," Journal of Public Social Services (December, 1970), p. 26.

167. W. Bateman, "Assessing Program Effectiveness," Welfare in Review (January-February, 1968), p. 2. See also, Hearings before the Committee on Education and Labor, House of Representatives, 90th Congress, First Session; or HR 8311, Economic Opportunity Act Amendments of 1967, Part II, pp. 1305-1317.

168. Bateman, op. cit., p. 8.

169. L. Ferman, Job Development for the Hard-to-Employ (Policy Papers in Human Resources and Industrial Relations, No. 11, A Joint Publication of the Institute of Labor and Industrial Relations of the University of Michigan and Wayne State University and the West Virginia University, 1969), pp. 18-19.

170. Briar, op. cit., p. 60.

171. See F. Hollis, Casework: A Psychosocial Theory (New York: Random House, 1965), p. 149.

172. A. Collins, The Lonely and Afraid (New York: The Odyssey Press, 1969), p. 6.

173. B. Reubens, The Hard-to-Employ: European Programs (New York: Columbia University Press, 1970), p. 5.

174. Collins, op. cit., p. 33.

175. Ibid., p. 137.

176. J. Mayer and N. Timms, The Client Speaks (New York: Atherton Press, 1970), p. 137.

177. Ibid.

178. Ibid., pp. 154-158. See also Parson's concept of "Functional Specificity" in The Motivation of Economic Activities," in Essays in Sociological Theory (New York: The Free Press, 1964), pp. 50-68.

179. R. Vinter, "Analysis of Treatment Organization," in Edwin Thomas (ed.), Behavioral Science for Social Workers (New York: The Free Press, 1967), p. 211.

180. Ibid., p. 220.

181. Mayer and Timms, op. cit., p. 137. See for instance the new ideas of "Amicatherapy," and "filial therapy."

182. Reubens, op. cit., p. 5.

183. M. Weber, "The Essentials of Bureaucratic Organization: An Ideal-Type Construction," in Robert K. Merton, et al. (ed.), Reader in Bureaucracy (Glencoe: The Free Press, 1952), pp. 18-27.

184. A. Gouldner, "Organizational Analysis," in Robert K. Merton, et al., Sociology Today (New York: Basic Books, Inc., 1959), p. 394.

185. Weber, op. cit., pp. 25-27.

186. M. Albrow, Bureaucracy (New York: Praeger Inc., 1970), p. 51.

187. Rosenheim, op. cit., pp. 140-144.

188. T. Parsons, Structure and Process in Modern Society (Glencoe: The Free Press, 1960).

189. Gouldner, op. cit., p. 394.

190. P. Blau, "Orientation Toward Clients in a Public Welfare Agency." In M. N. Zald (ed.), Social Welfare Institutions (New York: John Wiley & Sons, Inc., 1965), p. 660.

62

191. H. Specht, "The Deprofessionalization of Social Work," _Social Work_ (March, 1972), 3-15.

192. P. Blau and R. Scott, _Formal Organizations: A Comparative Approach_ (San Francisco: Chandler Publishing Co., 1962). The four types of organizations are: Mutual Benefit, Business, Service and Commonwealth.

193. Albrow, op. cit., p. 120.

194. See, for example, Blau and Scott, op. cit., pp. 165-193; P. Selznik, _Leadership in Administration_; E. Katz and S. N. Eisenstadt, "Bureaucracy and its Clientele: A Case Study," in A. Etzioni (ed.), _Readings in Modern Organizations_ (Englewood Cliffs, N.J.: Prentice Hall, Inc., 1969).

195. See, for instance, _Implementing Welfare-Employment Programs: An Institutional Analysis of the Work Incentive (WIN) Program_, cited above. In this study high performance in WIN was associated with the clarity of orientation by the leadership and staff as to orientation to the program goals.

196. Katz and Eisenstadt, op. cit., pp. 232-234; see also E. Thomas' "Role Concept" or Gouldner's concept of "Latent Identity."

197. R. K. Merton, _Social Theory and Social Structure_, revised edition (London: The Free Press of Glencoe, 1964), p. 369.

198. E. J. Thomas, "Problems of Disability from the Perspective of Role Therapy," in _Behavioral Sciences for Social Workers_, E. J. Thomas, Editor, op. cit., p. 70.

CHAPTER III

APPROACH TO THE STUDY

This study is basically a survey in that it tests hypotheses regarding the correlations between enrollees and staff perceptions of the WIN program. Specifically, the attempt has been to establish an ex post facto comparison of the perceptions of the WIN participants regarding the services provided by, and experienced in the WIN office. The ultimate aim has been to assess whether the supportive services of the WIN program significantly contribute to the enrollees' succeeding in, or dropping out of the program.

Hypotheses

The above goal has been sought because the thesis of this study is that the sustaining forces that influence the WIN enrollee's engagement in her training lie within the experiences offered by the interpersonal contacts with the WIN personnel, the variety of the supportive services, and the nature of their delivery, and not within any personal characteristic of the enrollee. It is thus first hypothesized that:

> There are no significant differences in demographic variables between Successes and Drop-Outs.

The review of the literature allows for the assumption that the helping process is successful when the worker is involved with, and is empathetic to the client; where there is worker-client congruence about the client's specific needs and the goals of their efforts; and when the institutional structure facilitates client-centered transactions. Therefore, an enrollee's success in the WIN program positively relates to the enrollee's agreement with the WIN worker regarding: assessment of the WIN services; perception of the enrollee's needs; evaluation of the WIN program goals; and description of the WIN office.

On the bases of the above, an overall hypothesis is as follows: Supportive services relate significantly to success in the WIN program. This is tested in 12 specific hypotheses noted below.

1. Successes--Drop-Outs

   a. There is a significant difference between the Successes' experiences with the WIN supportive services and the Drop-Outs' experiences with the WIN supportive services.

   b. There is a significant difference between the Successes' perception of their needs and the Drop-Outs' perception of their needs.

   c. There is a significant difference between the Successes' perception of the goals of the WIN program and the Drop-Outs' perception of the goals of the WIN program.

   d. There is a significant difference between the Successes' perception of the WIN office and the Drop-Outs' perception of the WIN office.

2. Successes--Staff

   a. There is no significant difference between the Staff's perception of the Successes' experiences with the WIN supportive services and the Successes' perception of their experiences with the WIN supportive services.

   b. There is no significant difference between the Staff's perception of the Successes' needs and the Successes' perception of their own needs.

   c. There is no significant difference between the Staff's perception of the goals of the WIN program and the Successes' perception of the goals of the WIN program.

   d. There is no significant difference between the Staff's description of the WIN office and the Successes' description of the WIN office.

3. Drop-Outs--Staff

   a. There is a significant difference between the Staff's perception of the Drop-Outs' experiences with the WIN supportive services and the Drop-Outs' perception of their experiences with the WIN supportive services.

b. There is a significant difference between the Staff's perception of the Drop-Outs' needs and the Successes' perception of their own needs.

c. There is a significant difference between the Staff's perception of the goals of the WIN program and the Drop-Outs' perception of the goals of the WIN program.

d. There is a significant difference between the Staff's description of the WIN office and the Drop-Outs' description of the WIN office.

The overall expectation is that the positive influence of the supportive services of the WIN program depends upon the existence of congruence between the perceptions of Staff and Successes in the four areas. It is not significant, it seems to me, whether this congruence existed upon the enrollee's entrance into the WIN program or developed in the course of the experience. Nor do I think that the worker can appreciate the total situation of the client at the moment of their first contact. I am expecting, however, that because of the client-worker congruence in all four areas at the end of the program, the Successes have had the benefit of supportive services. Parenthetically, one may comment that, since all WIN enrollees are, at least theoretically, voluntary referrals and have all been through the same screening procedures, they should all share in their perception of the WIN goals. However, as this is an _ex post facto_ study, it is reasonable to expect that the frustration of failure would have added this negative evaluation.

Population

The population of this study is drawn from the Phoenix WIN office. According to the directives of functional analysis,[1] the quality of a rendered service must be evaluated both from the perspective of the receiver as well as that of the agent who provides the service. This is the reason for seeking the perspectives of both WIN staff and enrollees. Moreover, as the emphasis of the study is not the particular work of each team or individual staff member, but rather the total context of the WIN experience, the aim of this research effort gears more to what Etzioni calls "a system model of evaluation."[2] Thus the population of this study consists of:

A. Administrative and line personnel.

There were four teams in the Phoenix WIN office at the time investigated by this study, each having four members. The administrative personnel of the office consisted of the manager, the manager's assistant, and the employment relations coordinator. Skill lab specialists and teachers raised the total number of staff to 24.

The following table gives the overall make-up of the Phoenix WIN office personnel at the time of the study.

Phoenix WIN Office Staff--by Position Size and Educational Background

Position	Number	Education
Administrative	3	M.S. in Counseling
Counselors	4	M.S. in Counseling
Vocational Education	1	M.S. in Vocational Education
	2	B.A.
Job Developers*	2	B.A.
All Others	12	High School Graduates

*A B.A. degree was not a requirement for the position of Job Developer.

Two staff members were deceased by the time this investigation was undertaken. The response of a third member had not been secured by the time the data were processed. Thus the actual sample of staff members is 21.

Parenthetically, it is worth noting that there has been practically no turnover of the WIN office staff during the program's first four years of operation. After the summer of 1972, two of the members involved in the program during the time investigated by this study left the state, one resigned to engage in local politics, and another was promoted to a higher administrative capacity within the State Employment Services. Changes occurred after 1978 when the original manager resigned and two more counselors moved into private practice.

B. Enrollees

The names of the enrollees were secured from a personality assessment study undertaken by Dr. Irwin Sandler of the Arizona State University faculty.[3] He interviewed the women at the end of the second week of their orientation, a condition that allows for the assumption that all respondents had been exposed to the same services during their initial contact with the WIN program. Only enrollees who entered the WIN program between September 1971 and January 1972 were included in the study.

There were approximately 30 to 35 women entering the WIN program every two weeks, making a total of 343 enrollees for the specific period of this study. Of those, 11 were duplications of the same women entering the program at two different times in the five month period. Another 7 women could not be identified, as they did not give their names to the Sandler study. Thus the total of the enrollee population was lowered to 325. It was established that 146 of these enrollees completed their employability plans, making the sample of successes 45% of the total population. The remaining 197 women, 55% of the total group, dropped out of the program before completion of their training.

It should be explained here that the terms of Success/Drop-Out are those of the WIN classification used at the time concerning this study. Success is the enrollee who completed her employability plan, i.e., placed on a job and remained employed for at least six months. Drop-Out is the enrollee who terminated before completion of her training. An effort to evaluate the reasons for termination of training was abandoned because it was not possible to establish an accurate conceptualization of the "legitimacy" of the termination. For instance, while the official termination of an enrollee may be given as "illness"--a legitimate reason--often the record left doubts about the enrollee's involvement with the program. Such an example would be the person who stated that she cannot continue participating because of illness, but neither the medical records nor the worker's contacts substantiated the claim. Also one could question why "personal problems" or "child care" have interfered with a certain enrollee's performance and not with the others. Therefore while the reasons for termination have been considered in the analysis of the demographics, they have not entered the assessment of the enrollee's status.

A desirable prerequisite in considering the enrollee population was that they (enrollees) should not have entered the WIN program during the initial year of its implementation, because it was felt that neither the philosophical nor the procedural frameworks of the program had been crystalized yet. It was also felt that the enrollees entering the program after the implementation of the Talmadge amendments should similarly be excluded, because the legislation had restricted the team members' field of activity. Therefore, enrollees "eligible" for this study were considered only those participating in the program between June 1970 and 1972. The selection sample falls within the specific period.

Another consideration in the choice of the enrollee sample was the fact that this specific group of the enrollees had undergone, upon their entry into the program, a variety of psychological tests--among them the Rotter I-E test for internal versus external control reinforcement and the Taylor Manifest Anxiety Scale.[4] Besides the obvious advantage of utilizing existing information, using the same population for the present study offered the exceptional opportunity to study the Phoenix WIN activity at its best. For as the WIN staff had the benefit of the Sandler's study data, they could presumably be facilitated in their helping tasks. An additional advantage was, as stated earlier, the assurance that all these enrollees went through the same steps during the first intensive two weeks of their training, an assurance which was supported both by the Sandler study design as well as the review of the enrollees' records.

No other efforts were made to match the Success and Drop-Out samples. Of course, in comparative studies the quest for exactitude may well be pursued further through more vigorous control procedures. However, in view of the size of the Phoenix WIN office, the volume of its activity and the problems of retrieval after practically a four year period, a desire for identical individual matching could not have yielded terminal groups of statistically satisfactory size. Besides, as Greenwood points out, we will never be able to identify all possible variables and reach absolute homogeneity of the population.[5] It seems legitimate, therefore, not to have sought strict precision control in sampling but rather maintain a balanced representation--a consideration that is adequately met by including in the sample the universe of enrollees within the specified period of these five months.

Responses were secured from 192 women: 98 of them Drop-Out and 94 Successes. However, 8 of the responses were collected after the data were computerized. It was felt that their influence would not be significant to the outcome of the study and therefore they are not included in the enrollee population. Thus the actual total of enrollees is 186, approximately 58% of the original population. It was ascertained that two enrollees were deceased and one was in prison. All three were Drop-Outs. Four additional enrollees refused to participate in the study. They represent equally the two studied groups. One of them, a Success, responded with a letter in which she gave her views of the WIN program, but she expressed disinterest in filling out the questionnaire.

To sum up, the final population upon which this study is based consists of 21 staff members and 186 enrollees. Of the latter group 91 or 49% are Successes, and 95 or 51% are Drop-Outs.

Data Gathering Procedures

A. Demographics

An almost automatic procedure, when we are faced with the relationship between two variables, is to consider the role of further variables in the observed outcome. In studies like the one discussed here, the quality of the outcome may well be influenced by the properties of the population. Thus it is obvious that the nature of the study requires cross tabulation of a variety of demographic factors between the Successes and Drop-Outs--the test of the first hypothesis.

Background information of the enrollee population was secured through the WIN files. Besides the traditional demographics of age, race, marital status, and number of dependents, the collected data thought of as relevant to this study include: education, history of employment, and length of time on welfare.

In working with the demographic variables, the chi-square test of statistical significance was used. The traditional .05 level of confidence was accepted. In addition, for those variables where there were ordinal values the averages and standard deviations were also computed.

In reviewing the enrollees' files, it became evident that information regarding the length of time an enrollee stayed in the WIN program and the reasons for terminating from it could add to our understanding of the value of the total WIN experience. Therefore these two variables were also compared, although they were not tested statistically.

B. Questionnaire

The main instrument of this study is a structured questionnaire which was prepared in parallel form for the enrollees and the WIN office personnel (see Appendix A). Following[6] is an account of the development of the questionnaire.

Item content. It has been well-established that effectiveness of services depends both on the appropriateness of their nature as well as on the system of their delivery. The great challenge in preparing the questionnaire was to identify the variables that best express the various dimensions of helpfulness, successful intervention, quality of effective services, and so on. An extensive review was made of studies investigating the helping process, both from the point of view of the helper as well as the recipient of help. Barrett-Lennard's inventory was a helpful starting point, as it offered not only a conceptual framework but also a procedural guideline in questionnaire formation. Five "helpful" qualities are identified as significant here. These are: empathic understanding and congruence of the therapist, his level of regard for the patient and the unconditionality of this regard, and his willingness to be known. In these positive dimensions these variables indicate that the helping person understands and empathizes with the client's experience, is purposefully and willingly involved with the client, has concern and respect for the client; and maintains all these conditions on a constant level.[7]

The above concepts of helpfulness have been substantiated by several studies. The need for expertise and knowledge, for instance, has been asserted in purely psychological studies,[8] as well as those examining social intervention.[9] So have the variables of motivation to help, concern for and involvement with the client, and availability to the client.[10]

The generic importance of exploring the actor's perceptions and view points has been well-recognized.[11] Thus, besides reviewing the literature for identification of relevant variables, a number of WIN workers as well as social workers were asked to suggest factors that, in their opinions contributed to effective intervention in a situation like the one under study. Again there was a consensus about the prerequisites of knowledge, motivation, self-involvement, concern, acceptance, open communication, and emphasis upon immediate reality of the situation.

Often in evaluative research the genuine concern to assess the client's opinion on the effectiveness of services is negated by the fact that the professionals originate the questionnaire items, thus limiting the preferences expressed through the research instrument. Carter, for instance, points out that there is often great discrepancy between what a worker reports as service delivered and what the recipient recognizes as such.[12] And Gottesfeld wonders whether new dimensions might have been present in a study of delinquency had the delinquents originated the item content of the questionnaire.[13] For this reason, an attempt was made to secure client input in the development of the questionnaire by asking present WIN enrollees what they thought was helping them with, or hindering them in their efforts. It is interesting to note that most of the WIN women responded with concrete examples of behavior on the part of the WIN staff rather than abstract qualitative descriptions. The conditions of being liked, being accepted as a person with unique needs, having a worker who is honest and who has the enrollee's concern at heart rather than the organization's, were most often mentioned as the ones promising success.

Similarly, the definition of enrollees' needs and the description of WIN goals are based on the literature and the populations' own statements.

Content Validation. Two attempts were made to validate the item content. First, the variables were defined, and the list of them was given to a number of colleagues of varying levels of experience, who then were asked to evaluate whether the questionnaire items were indicators of the defined variables. Following

73

this, the questionnaire--refined on the basis of significant suggestions--was pretested on a group of enrollees who have recently entered the WIN program. There has been basic agreement that the questionnaire items are indeed pertinent to the enrollees' experiences with, and concerns regarding, the WIN program.

Form. The above mentioned experience with the WIN enrollees was the basic reason for choosing a multiple-choice questionnaire form where some of the described experiences could be reproduced. An additional reason was the advantage it has of minimizing comparisons of answers to "related" items and, of course, the relative economy of its administration. As finally developed, the questionnaire has a total of forty (40) questions, equally divided into four parts: perception of experiences; perception of enrollees' needs; perception of program goals; and perception of the climate of operations in the WIN office.

Scoring method. The scoring procedure adopted involves weighting of the numerical answer categories and allows every answer to the items of a given variable to either add or detract from the resulting score. Specifically, the scoring method was as follows:

Part I   - Perception of Experiences
             There are 10 items each scoring from 4
             to 1, with the total score ranging from
             40 to 10. The items were scored on a
             continuum from positive to negative,
             with the highest score representing the
             most positive perception.

Part II   - Perception of Needs
             There are 10 items scored 4 to 1, giving a total range from 40 to 10. The
             items were scored on a continuum from
             positive to negative, with the highest
             score representing the most positive
             perception.

Part III   - Perception of Goals
             There are 10 items (scrambled) with
             scores ranging from 20 to -20. Items
             21, 22, 24, 27, and 29 were scored on a
             continuum from positive to negative,
             with the highest score representing the

most positive perception. The weighting order was reversed for the
remaining items.

Part IV - Perception of Operations
There are 10 items, each scoring from 4
to 1, with the total score ranging from
40 to 10. The items were scored on a
continuum from positive to negative,
with the highest score representing the
most positive perception.

Computation of the multivariate analysis of variance
was made through planned (orthogonal) contrasts.
Three such contrasts were performed: Staff-Successes;
Staff-Drop-Outs; and Successes-Drop-Outs. Thus, we
have three sets of statistical comparisons regarding
four dependent variables. To test the statistical
significance, the level of confidence was set at the
.05 conventional value.

Validity scales. One aspect of the validity problem
is the question of whether the primary data are themselves valid--in the sense that they reflect the
subject's direct conscious experience rather than, for
example, indicating how the manager would have liked
the staff to respond, or what the enrollee thought
would have pleased the counselor. Precautions that
were taken against such tendencies included telling
subjects truthfully that WIN personnel would not see
the answers and that the investigator was not con-
nected in any professional capacity with the WIN
administering department. Especially for the staff,
anonymity was secured through the provision of a
depository for the completed questionnaires. Specifically, the staff were asked to return the
questionnaires to a designated envelope in the cabinet
used to store the investigator's material. Thus,
except for the two mailed questionnaires, there is no
way of knowing the subject's identity.

There are two additional considerations that may raise
questions regarding the validity of the scales. The
first is the time lapse between the experience of the
subjects and the report of their experience. One may
wonder whether responses collected four years later
accurately report the transactions of the investigated
period. The second is the influence of later events
which could impinge upon the feelings of the respondents and color their impressions. For the enrollees,
for instance, success or failure with the program, or

ability to hold a job, might seriously affect their evaluation of the WIN experience. For the staff, the frustrations of the drastic changes in the exercise of their functions brought about by the Talmadge amendments could have affected a nostalgia for "the good old times" and thus have romanticized their perspicuity of "the way we were," so to speak.

The main precaution against the above influences was to share with the respondents the investigator's concern and to clarify that the focus of the study was the WIN experience of the time of its happening. That is, how they felt about the goals of the WIN program at that time, not now, and so on. Above all, efforts were made to ensure that both staff and enrollees understood that the value of the data for research purposes depended on the extent to which it represented their actual perceptions of the WIN experience.

Collection of data. The investigator collected the data herself. The staff questionnaires were delivered in person. Before delivery the investigator had met with the entire staff. At that time the study was explained to them, and their support was solicited.

The questionnaire was mailed to all enrollees along with a letter explaining the purpose of the study and requesting their assistance. A stamped, self-addressed envelope was enclosed. A second reminder letter was sent two weeks later to those who did not respond and whose first mailing did not return undelivered. A total of 82 enrollees returned their questionnaires by mail. The rest of the responses were secured through personal interviews by the investigator.

The addresses of the enrollees were secured through: the files of the WIN office; the files of the Department of Economic Security--for ADC and food stamps recipients; residents' lists of public housing projects; files of other training programs; hospitals' personnel files for employees; and other individual employers, as they were indicated in the enrollee's WIN file. It is worth noting that a number of respondents were secured through other enrollees who had maintained contact and who expressed interest in facilitating this research project.

76

C. Descriptive Information

It has been pointed out[14] that in conditional relationships often hypothesis testing is not enough to
assess the examined situation. The outcome of the
testing may support the original statement but does
not necessarily explain it. Besides the technical
limitations of the experimental design, there is what
Opton calls the "artificiality of outside interviewers" which may "block the potential of outside
interviews at a level somewhat better than superficial
but far less than ideal."[15] Opton's own study indicated that "research by outside interviewers must be
supplemented by inside research of the participant-
observer and/or anthropological model,"[16] in order to
have a more realistic appraisal of the existing relationships.

Such a caution is even more valid in studies like this
one where an objective instrument cannot capture the
actual transactions between enrollees and WIN personnel. As such transactions form the very thesis of the
study's argument, efforts were made to secure vignettes and other narrative material which could yield
descriptive information of the particular situations,
interactions, feelings, and other phenomena of the WIN
world, so to speak.

The above data were collected through interviews with
staff and enrollees. Through the letter sent with the
questionnaire, the enrollees were asked whether there
were other elements of their WIN experience which the
questionnaire did not cover and which they wished to
communicate to the investigator. The letter provided
for their answer. Of the 82 enrollees who returned
the questionnaire by mail, 34 expressed interest in
meeting with the investigator. Another 6 included
letters or written comments along with the questionnaire. One enrollee sent a written evaluation of the
WIN program but no questionnaire.

More than one-third of those enrollees interested in
discussing further their experiences with the WIN
could not be reached at the time of the inquiry. This
did not raise great concern because, as the majority
of the responses to the questionnaires were secured
through personal interviews, the descriptive data were
sought at the time of the interviews. A total of 104
enrollees were thus seen, 50 Successes, and 54 Drop-
Outs.

77

Although no statistical test of the interview material was attempted, attention was paid to the enrollee's status. Comparisons between responses of Successes and Drop-Outs were made both in descriptions of services and communicated feelings. Overall, however, the value of the narrative data remains in their descriptive nature, in the sense that they broaden our understanding of the transactions that form the WIN experience and provide models for the planning of similar services.

It must be noted that the effort to trace enrollees provided a serendipitous third source of descriptive data, namely, persons who worked with WIN enrollees and staff. Such persons include relatives of the enrollees, hospital personnel officials, nursing directors, nurses in charge of hospital nurses' and nurse's aides' programs, and officials of other training programs. This material is seen as having only a supportive value, in that it may confirm or qualify the data already collected. Perhaps a parenthetical benefit may be found in the directives such data may imply regarding the planning of follow-up services and the coordination of training and supportive services in manpower programs. Therefore, no analysis of these data has been attempted; their presence in this study is limited to a mere report.

FOOTNOTES

CHAPTER III

1. R. K. Merton, Social Theory and Social Structure, revised edition (London: The Free Press of Glencoe, 1964), pp. 50-54.

2. A. Etzioni, "Two Approaches to Organizational Analysis: A Critique and a Suggestion," Administrative Quarterly, 5:2 (September 1960), pp. 257-278.

3. I. Sandler, et al., Client Versus Staff Perceptions of the Interpersonal Characteristics of Welfare Recipients in a Manpower Development Program (mimeographed manuscript), 1973.

4. The tests were part of Dr. Sandler's study, op. cit.

5. E. Greenwood, <u>Experimental Sociology--A Study Method</u> (New York: King's Crown Press, 1945), pp. 78-91.

6. The idea of reporting my steps in this way was inspired by G. T. Barrett-Lennard, "Dimensions of Therapist Response as Causal Factors in Therapeutic Change," <u>Psychological Monographs: General and Applied</u>, 76:43 (Whole No. 562, 1962).

7. For Barrett-Lennard's own interpretations, see Ibid., pp. 3-6.

8. See, for instance, F. E. Fiedler's "A Comparative Investigation of early therapeutic relationships created by experts and non-experts of the psychoanalytic non-directive and Adlerian schools," <u>Journal of Consulting Psychology</u>, Vol. 14 (1950), pp. 435-445, or even Barrett-Lennard's own study.

9. For a number of such studies see "The Interview and Social Research," edited by David Riessman and Mark Benny, in the special issue of <u>American Journal of Sociology</u>, Vol. 62 (September 1956).

10. Just to list some examples of such studies: E. Thomas, et al., "The Expected Behavior of a Potentially Helpful Person," <u>Human Relations</u>, 8:2 (1955), pp. 165-174; M. Worby, op. cit., Manford Kuhn, "The Interview and the Professional Relationship," in <u>Human Behavior and Social Processes</u>, A. Rose, Editor, pp. 193-206; L. Ripple, <u>Motivation, Capacity, and Opportunity</u>, Social Service Monographs, The School of Social Service Administration, University of Chicago, 1964; J. Mayer and N. Timms, <u>The Client Speaks</u> (New York: Atherton Press, 1970).

11. See, for instance, Allen Barton and Paul Lazarsfeld, "Some Functions of Qualitative Analysis in Social Research," Reprint No. 18, Bureau of Applied Social Research, Columbia University; quoted in Mayer and Timms, op. cit., pp. 12-13.

12. G. Carter, "The Challenge of Accountability--How We Measure the Outcomes of Our Efforts," <u>Public Welfare</u>, Vol. 29, No. 3 (Summer 1971), pp. 267-277.

13. H. Gottesfeld, "Professionals and Delinquents Evaluate Professional Methods with Deliquents," <u>Social Problems</u>, Vol. 13, No. 1 (Summer 1965), p. 57.

14. E. Opton, <u>Factors Associated with Employment Among Welfare Mothers</u> (Berkeley: The Wright Institute, 1971); Merton, op. cit., pp. 93-94.

15. Opton, p. 188.

16. Ibid.

CHAPTER IV

AN INSIDE VIEW OF THE WIN PROGRAM

The basic argument of this study is that the supportive services of the WIN program are the primary
determinants of an enrollee's successful completion of
her training. It has been postulated that the rate of
influence of supportive services upon an enrollee
depends on the degree of the enrollee's congruence
with the staff on perceptions of: the experiences an
enrollee has with the WIN personnel; the enrollee's
needs; the goals of the WIN program; and the climate
of operations in the WIN office. It has been hypothesized that there would be no difference between Staff
and Successes on all four areas, while the Drop-Outs
would differ both from Staff and Successes on these
areas.

Assessment of the above has been attempted both
through hypotheses testing as well as through anecdo-
tal and other descriptive information. The former was
made through the use of a structured questionnaire
while the latter was secured through open-ended interviews with staff and enrollees. The findings,
therefore, are discussed separately.

The above argument has been based on the contention
that demographic factors play no important role in the
enrollee's success or dropping out of the program.
Assessment of demographic differences was sought
through hypothesis testing. Because of the relevance
of these findings to the interpretation of the questionnaire, their analysis will precede the discussion
of all other data.

Demographics

It has often been argued that a certain relationship
observed among two variables for a total sample may
hold in different degrees among various subgroups of
that sample. In order, therefore, to make valid in-
ferences from the main findings of this study, it was
first sought to ascertain whether there are any significant differences in the demographics of the
enrollees. The demographics selected for the testing
of the first hypothesis are: ethnicity, marital status, age, number of dependents, education, employment

history, and length of period on welfare. The information was secured through the WIN files and represents the status of the enrollee at the time she entered the WIN program.

Table 1 indicates the ethnic make-up of the enrollee population. As the ethnicity of one Success enrollee was not known, she was eliminated from the group for this comparison.

TABLE 1

ETHNIC CHARACTERISTICS OF THE
ENROLLEE POPULATION

Ethnicity	Successes N=88[a]	Drop-Outs N=95
White	46 (51%)	35 (37%)
Mexican-Americans	18 (20%)	23 (24%)
Blacks	21 (24%)	35 (37%)
American-Indians	3 (3%)	2 (2%)

df = 3
X^2 = 5.62
p > .05

[a]Two Successes have been eliminated from this computation because they did not belong to any of the above categories and their frequency was too small to warrant attention.

From the percentages alone it seems that the Drop-Out sample has a higher number of Blacks and fewer Whites than the Success group. However, the probability value of .10 is beyond the established level of significance set for the study at the traditional value of .05.

The findings for marital status are clearer as is shown on Table 2. Again, the probability value of .20 indicates that there is no significant difference between Successes and Drop-Outs in marital status at the time of their enrollment in the WIN program.

Table 3 indicates the age of the enrollees when they entered WIN. It is perhaps interesting to note that the Drop-Out group has a considerably higher percentage of women in the 15-19 years old bracket. On the other hand no significant difference is seen in the number of dependents each enrollee group has, as is shown in Table 4.

TABLE 2

MARITAL STATUS OF THE ENROLLEES

Marital Status	Successes N=91	Drop-Outs N=94
Never married	25 (27%)	36 (38%)
Ever married	66 (73%)	58 (62%)

$df = 1$
$X^2 = 2.43$
$p > .05$

TABLE 3

AGE OF THE ENROLLEES AT THE TIME OF THEIR ENTRY
IN THE WIN PROGRAM

Age	Successes N=91	Drop-Outs N=95
15-19 years	11 (12%)	20 (21%)
20-24 years	29 (32%)	30 (32%)
25-29 years	21 (23%)	18 (19%)
30-34 years	13 (14%)	14 (15%)
35-39 years	7 (8%)	6 (6%)
40-44 years	6 (7%)	4 (4%)
45 or older	4 (4%)	3 (3%)
M	25.8 years	25.9 years
SD	7.9 years	7.6 years

TABLE 4

NUMBER OF CHILDREN THE ENROLLEES HAD WHEN THEY ENTERED THE WIN PROGRAM

Number of children	Successes N=91		Drop-Outs N=95	
None	3	(3%)	7	(7%)
1	28	(31%)	26	(27%)
2	26	(28%)	20	(21%)
3	11	(12%)	19	(20%)
4	6	(7%)	11	(12%)
5	8	(9%)	9	(10%)
6	7	(8%)	1	(1%)
7	2	(2%)	2	(2%)
M	2.6		2.5	
SD	1.8		1.8	

Again, as seen in Table 5, there seems to be a considerably higher percentage of Drop-Outs who had completed high school education by the time they entered WIN, a fact that appears contrary to expectations for a manpower training program. It has been argued, for instance, that one of the impediments in the vocational preparation of women on welfare is their limited educational background. One would, therefore, assume that high school completion gives a WIN trainee a headstart over the others, especially as the high school diploma or its equivalent has usually been the first step in the WIN training.

TABLE 5

EDUCATIONAL LEVEL REACHED BY THE ENROLLEES AT THE TIME THEY ENTERED THE WIN PROGRAM (Last year completed)

Educational Level	Successes N=91	Drop-Outs N=95
Up to 8th grade	22 (24%)	18 (19%)
9th-11th grades	38 (43%)	39 (41%)
High School graduate	26 (28%)	37 (39%)
Attended some college	5 (5%)	1 (1%)

Median category for both groups: 9th-11th grades.

Neither prior employment history (Table 6) nor length of period an enrollee had been on welfare (Table 7) appear to be of major importance to whether she succeeded in, or dropped out from the WIN program.

TABLE 6

EMPLOYMENT HISTORY OF THE ENROLLEES PRIOR TO
THEIR ENTERING THE WIN PROGRAM

Employment History	Successes N=91	Drop-Outs N=95
None	20 (22%)	37 (39%)
Under 1 year	26 (29%)	18 (19%)
1-2 years	18 (20%)	16 (17%)
3-5 years	22 (24%)	23 (24%)
6 years or more	5 (5%)	1 (1%)

Median category for both groups: Under 1 year.

TABLE 7

LENGTH OF TIME ENROLLEES HAD BEEN ON WELFARE
WHEN THEY ENTERED THE WIN PROGRAM

Time on Welfare	Successes N=91	Drop-Outs N=95
Under 6 months	17 (19%)	27 (29%)
6-12 months	30 (33%)	26 (28%)
13-18 months	10 (11%)	6 (6%)
19-24 months	4 (4%)	8 (8%)
25-36 months	12 (13%)	7 (7%)
37-48 months	3 (3%)	5 (5%)
49-60 months	6 (7%)	3 (3%)
Over 60 months	7 (8%)	13 (14%)
Not known	2 (2%)	
M	19.7 months	21 months
SD	17.7 months	19.5 months

Actually none of these demographics played a decisive role in the enrollee's involvement with WIN. As

stated earlier the chi-square test of statistical
significance was used. The results of the test for
each relationship are shown in Table 8. It can be
seen that none of the five variables tested showed
differences between the two groups.

TABLE 8

TESTS OF SIGNIFICANCE FOR DIFFERENCES BETWEEN
SUCCESSES AND DROP-OUTS ON FIVE DEMOGRAPHIC VARIABLES

Demographic Variables	x^2	df	p
Age	3.1	6	>.05
No. of Dependents	10.0	7	>.05
Education	4.8	3	>.05
Prior Employment	9.2	4	>.05
Length of Time on Welfare	9.2	7	>.05

It is safe to assume that these demographic variables
do not predict successful completion of the WIN program or dropping-out of it for this matter. One may,
however, want to venture to explain some of the apparent variations in the population characteristics
between the two groups of enrollees. For instance,
one could see the higher percentage of never-married
Drop-Outs as related to the higher percentage of 15-19
year olds among the same group. The same relationship
may be ascribed to the higher presence of women with
no work experience among those who dropped out of the
WIN program. One also could relate the higher
percentage of high-school graduates in the Drop-Out
sample to the larger number of Blacks in that status
group. Such a finding corresponds with national
statistics which clearly indicate that there are more
Black high school graduates than any other minority
group.

The following two tables are of supplemental value
rather than of direct significance to the study. Table 9 gives the length of time the enrollees stayed in
the WIN program. This is rather descriptive information, and no statistical test of comparison has been
attempted. Nor has there been any effort made to
differentiate how many of the women were placed on a

job at the time they dropped out of the program. For the Successes, the time variable indicates at least six months of employment as their EPC (Employability Plan Completed) status implies, by definition, a six-month follow-up after satisfactory job placement.

As the emphasis of this study is the effect of supportive services, it is interesting to note that the Successes have stayed longer in WIN than the Drop-Outs. With an average length of more than 52 weeks, the Successes have definitely been the recipients of quantitatively higher doses of WIN services. If support builds on support, one may assume from these findings that the Successes have enjoyed the accelerated benefits of a sustained enabling experience. On the other hand an average stay of less than 27 weeks places the Drop-Outs in a disadvantaged position in terms of accumulated benefits from WIN services.

TABLE 9

LENGTH OF TIME ENROLLEES STAYED
IN THE WIN PROGRAM

Length in WIN	Successes N=91		Drop-Outs N=95	
Under 4 weeks	-		1	(1%)
5-12 weeks	3	(3%)	9	(9%)
13-26 weeks	9	(10%)	34	(37%)
27-39 weeks	22	(24%)	32	(34%)
40-52 weeks	23	(25%)	9	(9%)
53-78 weeks	26	(29%)	9	(9%)
Over 79 weeks	8	(9%)	1	(1%)

The last table in this group (Table 10) gives the reasons for enrollee termination with the program. As the reason for the Successes was the completion of their employability plan, only Drop-Outs are presented in this table. Again this information is only descriptive. The stated reasons are the ones given in the enrollee's record and no evaluation is made as to whether they represent the actual cause of the enrollee's dropping-out or a euphemism for it.

TABLE 10

REASONS FOR THE DROP-OUTS' TERMINATION OF THEIR WIN TRAINING

Reasons for Termination	Drop-Outs
Lack of interest	26 (28%)
Personal problems	8 (8%)
Health problems	15 (16%)
Pregnancy	7 (7%)
Marriage	8 (8%)
Moved from area	9 (10%)
Other training program	10 (11%)
Higher education	4 (4%)
Other	8 (8%)

Lack of interest seems by far the most frequent reason for enrollee dropping out of WIN, accounting for practically one-third of the total Drop-Out population. This finding, combined with those from the demographics and the questionnaire, may lead to a number of interpretations in terms of the synergistic effects of a variety of factors. However, the immediate reaction to the information given in this table is one of surprise. The reaction is based on the original assumption of this study that one's voluntary enrollment and continuing with the program past the initial two weeks of intensive orientation imply at least an adequate interest in the program. Therefore, the high percentage of those who dropped out because of "lack of interest" suggests some failure in the system of supportive services to reach a certain population. The discussion of the open-ended interviews allows for some insight as to the factors that contribute to the above outcome.

Analysis of the Questionnaire

As it was explained in the previous chapter, the questionnaire consists of forty questions divided equally into the four studied areas: experiences, needs, goals, and operations. Although in the ensuing discussion of each of these areas attention will be paid to individual items, it must be remembered that no one variable should be considered of sufficient influence

alone.   This caution does not necessarily mean that
certain predominant factors may not be operating to
produce a given problem in an enrollee's engagement in
her training.   It simply means that, even if we select
a given factor as primary, our understanding of the
effect of supportive services will not be furthered
unless we assess this factor in relationship to the
entire complex of factors operating at a given time.

1.   Experiences.   The first part of the questionnaire
deals with possible experiences an enrollee may have
had with the WIN personnel.   The respondent is given a
set of descriptions of transactions between enrollees
and staff and is asked to choose from one of four
possible answers ranging from very positive to very
negative.   The degree of helpfulness of these transactions is defined by the positiveness of the response.

Table 11 presents the responses of each of the three
study groups to the items relating to the perception
of the experiences an enrollee has with the WIN
personnel.   As the responses are descriptive rather
than of the agree/disagree type, each item is
presented separately along with the comparative
answers of each group.   However, in order to capture
the total picture of each group's perceptions of the
enrollee's experiences, three additional tables were
prepared in which each population's responses to the
experiences factor are given.   These tables (12, 13,
and 14) have number and letter designations for the
items and responses respectively.

It is obvious that the staff members feel very positive about their involvement with the WIN enrollees,
or, at least, they see themselves as having been concerned with, and helpful to, their clients (Table 12).
Perhaps it should be noted that the highest score of
positive response is reached on Item 4.   This item
deals with the Staff's reaction when faced with personal questions by the enrollees.   Eighty-six percent
(86%) of the Staff gave an a response, that is, the
worker "answered the question simply and directly,"
while the remaining fourteen percent (14%) responded
that the worker "avoided a direct answer but refocused
on the enrollee," a b response.   It is interesting
that the same item also scores highest in the responses of both Successes and Drop-Outs as Tables 13 and 14
indicate.

TABLE 11

PERCEPTION OF EXPERIENCES AN ENROLLEE HAS WITH THE WIN PERSONNEL

Item 1. During the course of an Enrollee's contact with the WIN, the Enrollee had the definite impression that the person assigned to her was:

	(a) Definitely interested in helping the Enrollee in all aspects of her life	(b) Mostly interested in helping the Enrollee to go through the program	(c) Mostly interested in getting higher work done	(d) Definitely not interested in helping the Enrollee	(e) No answer
Staff N=21	14 (67%)	7 (33%)			
Successes N=91	76 (84%)	13 (14%)	2 (2%)		
Drop-Outs N=95	63 (67%)	23 (24%)		7 (7%)	2 (2%)

Item 2. While at the WIN, the Enrollee felt that the person assigned to her:

	(a) Was deeply concerned that the Enrollee become a happier person in every respect	(b) Was deeply concerned that the Enrollee become financially independent so that she could go off welfare	(c) Was deeply concerned that the Enrollee succeed in the program so that he/she has another success to his/her credit	(d) Did not care at all whether the Enrollee felt happy or not	(e) No answer
Staff N=21	11 (52%)	10 (48%)			
Successes N=91	61 (67%)	26 (29%)	4 (4%)		
Drop-Outs N=95	50 (53%)	28 (30%)	7 (7%)	8 (8%)	2 (2%)

Item 3. When an Enrollee reported her problems to the WIN person assigned to her, he/she:

	(a) Accepted them as important and was able to assist the Enrollee with them	(b) Accepted them as important and volunteered to help the Enrollee if she needed any assistance	(c) Did not consider them serious enough to require higher involvement	(d) Consider them insignificant	(e) No answer
Staff N=21	6 (29%)	15 (71%)			
Successes N=91	38 (42%)	49 (54%)	3 (3%)		1 (1%)
Drop-Outs N=95	32 (34%)	46 (48%)	10 (11%)	5 (5%)	2 (2%)

Item 4. Whenever an Enrollee asked the WIN person assigned to her a question about his/her own life, he/she:

	(a) Answered the question simply and directly	(b) Avoided a direct answer but refocused on the Enrollee	(c) Indicated that the question was not relevant to their work	(d) Answered grudgingly	(e) No answer
Staff N=21	18 (86%)	3 (14%)			
Successes N=91	79 (88%)	5 (5%)	2 (2%)		5 (5%)
Drop-Outs N=95	68 (72%)	8 (8%)	9 (10%)	3 (3%)	7 (7%)

Item 5. In times of trouble, the WIN person assigned to the Enrollee:

	(a) Was sympathetic and practical in the solutions he/she suggested	(b) Was sympathetic and offered to help the Enrollee if she needed any assistance	(c) He/she told the Enrollee what she should do	(d) Offered neither sympathy nor solutions	(e) No answer
Staff N=21	6 (29%)	15 (71%)			
Successes N=91	33 (36%)	50 (56%)	5 (5%)	1 (1%)	2 (2%)
Drop-Outs N=95	28 (30%)	48 (51%)	8 (8%)	9 (9%)	2 (2%)

TABLE 11 (continued)

Item 6. Here is a made up example. Let us say that one day the Enrollee had car trouble and she telephoned to report that she could not go to the WIN office that day. What do you think the WIN person assigned to her would do:

	(a) Help the Enrollee make possible arrangements so that she could go to the WIN office that day and/or in the future	(b) Suggests possible ways for the Enrollee to go to the WIN office	(c) Insist that the Enrollee find a way to go to the WIN office	(d) Express doubt about the truthfulness of the Enrollee's reason	(e) No answer
Staff N=21	10 (48%)	11 (52%)			
Successes N=91	70 (77%)	16 (18%)	5 (5%)		
Drop-Outs N=95	62 (66%)	20 (21%)	4 (4%)	7 (7%)	2 (2%)

Item 7. Another made up example. Let us say an Enrollee had trouble with her ex-husband or sick children, or someone else in the family, and she was so upset that she could not do well in her training. What do you think the WIN person assigned to her would do:

	(a) Made it possible for the Enrollee to continue attending the program while helping her handle her problem	(b) Sympathize with the Enrollee and express understanding that she needs to take some time off from the program so that she can handle her personal problems	(c) Insist that the Enrollee must continue attending the WIN program because her training should have priority	(d) Question the Enrollee's motivation for training since she allows personal and family troubles to interfere with her work	(e) No answer
Staff N=21	15 (71%)	6 (29%)			
Successes N=91	59 (65%)	21 (24%)	4 (4%)	4 (4%)	3 (3%)
Drop-Outs N=95	50 (53%)	32 (34%)	5 (5%)	5 (5%)	3 (3%)

Item 8. If one day an Enrollee failed to show up in the WIN office the WIN person assigned to her would:

	(a) Call the Enrollee to find out whether he/she could be of help	(b) Be interested enough to call the Enrollee and see what was the matter	(c) Call the Enrollee and complain about her failing to show up	(d) Not bother to call the Enrollee	(e) No answer
Staff N=21	7 (33%)	13 (62%)		1 (5%)	
Successes N=91	28 (31%)	50 (56%)	3 (3%)	7 (7%)	3 (3%)
Drop-Outs N=95	28 (30%)	42 (44%)	6 (6%)	10 (11%)	9 (9%)

Item 9. If something in the way an Enrollee looked (or believed) could interfere with her preparing for a job, the WIN person assigned to her would:

	(a) Help the Enrollee make the needed changes	(b) Suggest to the Enrollee that perhaps some changes are needed	(c) Tell the Enrollee to change her appearance (behavior)	(d) Criticize the Enrollee about the way she looks (behaves)	(e) No answer
Staff N=21	6 (29%)	15 (71%)			
Successes N=91	52 (57%)	35 (39%)	2 (2%)	1 (1%)	1 (1%)
Drop-Outs N=95	42 (44%)	40 (43%)	2 (2%)	5 (5%)	6 (6%)

Item 10. While at the WIN office whenever an Enrollee needed any assistance:

	(a) There was always someone available to help her	(b) There was usually someone around whom an Enrollee could talk to	(c) An Enrollee had to find someone from her team to talk to	(d) An Enrollee had to wait until an appointment was scheduled for her with a team member	(e) No answer
Staff N=21	6 (29%)	13 (62%)	2 (8%)		
Successes N=91	56 (62%)	22 (24%)	8 (9%)	5 (5%)	
Drop-Outs N=95	50 (53%)	21 (22%)	13 (14%)	6 (6%)	5 (5%)

TABLE 12

STAFF'S PERCEPTION OF THE EXPERIENCES AN
ENROLLEE HAS WITH THE WIN PERSONNEL

N=21

Items	a	b	c	d	No answer
1	14 (67%)	7 (33%)			
2	11 (52%)	10 (48%)			
3	6 (29%)	15 (71%)			
4	18 (86%)	3 (14%)			
5	6 (29%)	15 (71%)			
6	10 (48%)	11 (52%)			
7	15 (71%)	6 (29%)			
8	7 (33%)	13 (62%)		1 (5%)	
9	6 (29%)	15 (71%)			
10	6 (29%)	13 (62%)	2 (8%)		

The value of this observation will become more clear
in the discussion of the open-ended interviews with
the enrollees. During these interviews many women
commented positively on the fact that the WIN staff
used themselves as examples and shared their own
personal experiences in child rearing and marital
situations and their ways of coping with them. Also
the fact that a number of WIN employees had themselves
been WIN trainees seemed to have a significant positive impact on the enrollees and, perhaps, on the
Staff's ability to be open and direct with their present clients.

The high score of the Staff's response to Item 7
(Tables 11 and 12) shows, perhaps, the Staff's determination to maintain the enrollees in their training,
or at least the value they place on this training.
Item 7 provides the respondents with a hypothetical
situation where personal difficulties upset the enrollee to the extent that she "could not do well" in
her training. The respondents are asked what would
the WIN worker do. Seventy-one percent (71%) of the
Staff answered that they would make it possible for
enrollees to continue while helping them to handle
their problem. The remaining 29% sympathized with the
enrollees and agreed that enrollees should take some
time off from the program so that they could attend to

their problem. None saw themselves critical of the enrollees or even indifferent to the enrollees' personal concerns.

TABLE 13

SUCCESSES' PERCEPTION OF THE EXPERIENCES AN
ENROLLEE HAS WITH THE WIN PERSONNEL

N=91

Items	a	b	c	d	No answer
1	76 (84%)	13 (14%)	2 (2%)		
2	61 (67%)	26 (29%)	4 (4%)		
3	38 (42%)	49 (54%)	3 (3%)		1 (1%)
4	79 (88%)	5 (5%)	2 (2%)		5 (5%)
5	33 (36%)	50 (56%)	5 (5%)	1 (1%)	2 (2%)
6	70 (77%)	16 (18%)	5 (5%)		
7	59 (65%)	21 (24%)	4 (4%)	4 (4%)	3 (3%)
8	28 (31%)	50 (56%)	3 (3%)	7 (7%)	3 (3%)
9	52 (57%)	35 (39%)	2 (2%)	1 (1%)	1 (1%)
10	56 (62%)	22 (24%)	8 (9%)	5 (5%)	

TABLE 14

DROP-OUTS' PERCEPTION OF THE EXPERIENCES AN
ENROLLEE HAS WITH THE WIN PERSONNEL

N=95

Items	a	b	c	d	No answer
1	63 (67%)	23 (24%)		7 (7%)	2 (2%)
2	50 (53%)	28 (30%)	7 (7%)	8 (8%)	2 (2%)
3	32 (34%)	46 (48%)	10 (11%)	5 (5%)	2 (2%)
4	68 (72%)	8 (8%)	9 (10%)	3 (3%)	7 (7%)
5	28 (30%)	48 (51%)	8 (8%)	9 (9%)	2 (2%)
6	62 (66%)	20 (21%)	4 (4%)	7 (7%)	2 (2%)
7	50 (53%)	32 (34%)	5 (5%)	5 (5%)	3 (3%)
8	28 (30%)	42 (44%)	6 (6%)	10 (11%)	9 (9%)
9	42 (44%)	40 (43%)	2 (2%)	5 (5%)	6 (6%)
10	50 (53%)	21 (22%)	13 (14%)	6 (6%)	5 (5%)

There is a greater variation in the responses of the enrollees to the same item (Tables 11, 13, and 14), although, here too, the overall impression is positive. In the same line of comparison the Staff's definite interest in helping the enrollee in all aspects of her life (Table 11) has the endorsement of only 67% of the WIN personnel. Similar is the reaction of the Drop-Outs. For the Successes this interest seems to have higher significance as 84% of them find their workers so interested. Actually, as Table 13 indicates, the overall assessment of the experiences by the Successes scores much more positive than that of the Staff. On the other hand, as seen in Table 14, the Drop-Outs rate their experiences much lower than either Successes or Staff. Nevertheless, even the Drop-Outs seem to think overall positively about the exchanges they have had with the WIN personnel. These findings allow for the assumption that both groups of enrollees benefited, or in some way were helped, by their transactions with the WIN staff, an assumption that, as seen earlier, is supported by similar findings in other research efforts.

2. Needs. Table 15 gives the Staff's perception of the enrollees needs at the time the latter entered the WIN program. These needs relate to the enrollee's limitations in social coping capacities which resulted from their disadvantaged situational context. Accurate recognition of such needs by both staff and enrollees could greatly facilitate the interventional process and guide its direction. Although not unanimous, the overall impression of the WIN staff members is that their clients' needs are significant indeed. Particularly high score items 11, 16, and 12 (in this order), all of which have to do with the enrollee's need for emotional support which would allow for the development of self-confidence. Interestingly enough, these needs are highly recognized by the enrollees as well (Tables 16 and 17), although neither Successes nor Drop-Outs respond as strongly to Item 11 which makes specific reference to the enrollee's fear to go to work. On the whole, though, both groups of enrollees perceive their needs much lower than the WIN staff.

These findings are interesting and, perhaps, crucial, especially since there is only a minor difference between the two enrollee groups. As it is shown in Table 17, the Drop-Outs object rather strongly to their being ascribed all these needs. Particularly they object to their being described as needing to learn how to get along with people (Item 18), how to control their tempers (Item 17), and how to handle their children (Item 19). The same items--and in the same order--raise the strongest objections from the Successes' group as well. One might tend to assume that these women see themselves more handicapped in relationship to the "outside" world, so to speak, but feel that they have been able to manage adequately in their immediate environment. Such an assumption is supported, or at least clarified, by the informal discussions with these women. During these interviews, their objections to these needs were not as strong because of the opportunity to qualify their statements.

3. Goals. The next ten items relate to the goals of the WIN program as these goals were perceived by Staff and enrollees at the time the latter entered the program. The items in this factor are scrambled, with Items 23, 25, 26, 28, and 30 ascribing to the WIN a negative purpose. In evaluating the score for this factor, the values of the responses to the above identified items were reversed in order to follow the same positive direction in the computation of the means. However, Tables 18, 19, and 20 present these scales uncorrected, so to speak, as they give the "raw" data of the responses.

Again, the Staff (Table 18) seem to see the goals of the WIN program as gearing to the welfare of the enrollees, although some 24% of them think that "saving the taxpayer money" is of "primary" concern. The responses of Successes and Drop-Outs, in Tables 19 and 20 respectively, show greater variation in their appraisal of the WIN goals. And, again, while the overall trend in both sets of answers is one of positive assessment, the Drop-Outs seem to feel less positive than the Successes. It is perhaps worth noting that 40% of Drop-Outs consider that the "primary" goal of the WIN program is to save the taxpayer money. Supported by some hindsight from the open-ended discussion, this response seems to reflect the client's basic mistrust of the "welfare" system whose programs do not evolve around the well-being of the poor people but rather around the interests of the privileged society. Yet, their emphatic refusal to agree with the other negative suggestions regarding

TABLE 15

STAFF'S PERCEPTION OF AN ENROLLEE'S NEEDS AT THE TIME OF HER ENTERING THE PROGRAM

"When an Enrollee entered the WIN program I felt that besides training she needed": N=21

Items	Strongly agree	Sonewhat agree	Somewhat disagree	Strongly disagree	No answer
11. Emotional support because she was scared to go to work	11 (52%)	9 (43%)		1 (5%)	
12. Help to stand on her own feet	5 (24%)	15 (71%)		1 (5%)	
13. To take some interest in her appearance	5 (24%)	10 (48%)		6 (28%)	
14. To learn how to schedule her day's work	8 (38%)	9 (43%)		4 (19%)	
15. Assistance with how to budget her money	3 (14%)	12 (57%)	5 (24%)	1 (5%)	
16. To build some confidence in herself	10 (48%)	10 (48%)	1 (4%)		
17. To learn to control her temper	2 (9%)	9 (43%)	10 (48%)		
18. To learn how to get along with people	7 (33%)	7 (33%)	5 (24%)		2 (10%)
19. Help with how to handle her children	7 (33%)	9 (43%)	5 (24%)		
20. To overcome her shyness	4 (19%)	11 (52%)	6 (29%)		

TABLE 16

SUCCESSES' PERCEPTION OF AN ENROLLEE'S NEEDS AT THE TIME OF HER ENTERING THE PROGRAM

"When I entered the WIN program I felt that besides training I needed":

N=91

Items	Strongly agree	Somewhat agree	Somewhat disagree	Strongly disagree	No answer
11. Emotional support because I was afraid to go to work	22 (24%)	27 (30%)	16 (18%)	24 (26%)	2 (2%)
12. Help to stand on my own feet	39 (43%)	38 (42%)	4 (4%)	10 (11%)	
13. To take some interest in my appearance	13 (14%)	30 (33%)	17 (19%)	30 (33%)	1 (1%)
14. To learn how to schedule my day's work	23 (25%)	22 (24%)	15 (17%)	29 (32%)	2 (2%)
15. Assistance with how to budget my own money	27 (30%)	23 (25%)	15 (17%)	23 (25%)	3 (3%)
16. To build some confidence in myself	55 (61%)	20 (22%)	9 (10%)	7 (7%)	
17. To learn to control my temper	14 (15%)	15 (17%)	15 (17%)	45 (49%)	2 (2%)
18. To learn how to get along with people	19 (21%)	22 (24%)	9 (10%)	40 (44%)	1 (1%)
19. Help with how to handle my children	13 (14%)	24 (26%)	19 (21%)	34 (38%)	1 (1%)
20. To overcome my shyness	29 (32%)	26 (29%)	13 (14%)	22 (24%)	1 (1%)

TABLE 17

DROP-OUTS' PERCEPTION OF AN ENROLLEE'S NEEDS AT THE TIME OF HER ENTERING THE PROGRAM

"When I entered the WIN program I felt that besides training I needed": N=95

Items	Strongly agree	Somewhat agree	Somewhat disagree	Strongly disagree	No answer
11. Emotional support because I was afraid to go to work	26 (28%)	20 (21%)	10 (10%)	33 (35%)	6 (6%)
12. Help to stand on my own feet	40 (43%)	23 (24%)	8 (8%)	22 (23%)	2 (2%)
13. To take some interest in my appearance	20 (21%)	21 (21%)	14 (15%)	35 (37%)	5 (5%)
14. To learn how to schedule my day's work	31 (31%)	25 (26%)	12 (13%)	24 (25%)	3 (3%)
15. Assistance with how to budget my own money	39 (41%)	21 (22%)	6 (6%)	27 (29%)	2 (2%)
16. To build some confidence in myself	49 (52%)	16 (17%)	8 (8%)	17 (18%)	5 (5%)
17. To learn to control my temper	19 (20%)	16 (17%)	14 (15%)	42 (44%)	4 (4%)
18. To learn how to get along with people	13 (14%)	21 (22%)	13 (14%)	43 (45%)	5 (5%)
19. Help with how to handle my children	20 (21%)	20 (21%)	9 (10%)	38 (40%)	8 (8%)
20. To overcome my shyness	26 (27%)	26 (27%)	7 (7%)	31 (34%)	5 (5%)

the WIN goals is an indication of their acceptance of a "difference" in the nature of this "welfare program." Experiences with WIN have reassured many of these enrollees of the reality of such a difference. So, perhaps, Item 23 represents a concession to a broader social value, that of the work ethic, and to the ensuring attitude that priority in governmental concerns is reserved for the deserving, wage-earning citizen. One may speculate even further and see this response as an additional attitude resulting from the same ethic, namely that governmental protection should come only in terms of saving taxes rather than in provision of services and other such guarantees.

4. Operations. The evaluation of the climate of operations of the WIN office provides an interesting twist to the up-to-now trend of responses. For in terms of raw data and percentages, this is the first factor in which the Staff scored lowest. Both groups of enrollees perceive the WIN office much more favorably than the WIN staff, although, again, there is an overall positive assessment of WIN's organizational atmosphere and function. For instance, while 77% of the Successes and 73% of the Drop-Outs (Tables 22 and 23 respectively) strongly agree that "the WIN office is a really nice place," only 38% of the Staff (Table 21) find it so. On the other hand all three groups tend to strongly agree that day care arrangements were an important factor in the WIN program and therefore it was of concern to both enrollees and staff. The descriptive material strongly supports this point. However, the other items are not accorded such unanimity. The Successes particularly feel that the Staff treated them as persons "with special needs and interests," and that their preferences were included in the selection of their employability plans. Drop-Outs, on the other hand, did not feel so attended to.

Perhaps the most interesting finding in the operations factor is the ambivalence of all involved regarding the evaluation of the WIN office as "a social service agency rather than a training school" (Item 40). The open-ended interviews offered some insight into the sources of the ambivalence, but they established the ambivalence even further. That is, while the Staff seemed to see their work as goal oriented, all services given being necessary but auxiliary to the preparation for employment, the enrollees seemed to emphasize the positive nature of the WIN office as

TABLE 18

STAFF'S PERCEPTION OF THE GOALS OF THE WIN PROGRAM

"As I understand it the WIN program was established in order to":

N=21

Items	Strongly agree	Somewhat agree	Somewhat disagree	Strongly disagree	No answer
21. Give women on welfare another chance in life	11 (52%)	10 (48%)			
22. Help welfare women become self-dependent	9 (43%)	12 (57%)			
23. Primarily save the tax-payer money	1 (5%)	4 (19%)	12 (57%)	3 (14%)	1 (5%)
24. Assist women on welfare get jobs of their choice	7 (33%)	13 (62%)	1 (5%)		
25. Force everyone to go to work		1 (5%)	5 (24%)	14 (66%)	1 (5%)
26. Make welfare women work for their keep		2 (10%)	6 (28%)	12 (57%)	1 (5%)
27. Help those who are able to move ahead in life	9 (43%)	12 (57%)			
28. Make the government look good			7 (33%)	14 (67%)	
29. Give welfare women the know-how of running their own lives	3 (14%)	12 (57%)	4 (19%)	1 (5%)	1 (5%)
30. Provide cheap labor for the big business			7 (33%)	14 (67%)	

TABLE 19

SUCCESSES' PERCEPTION OF THE GOALS OF THE WIN PROGRAM

"As I understand it the WIN program was established in order to":

N=91

Items	Strongly agree	Somewhat agree	Somewhat disagree	Strongly disagree	No answer
21. Give women on welfare another chance in life	75 (83%)	11 (12%)	4 (4%)		1 (1%)
22. Help welfare women become self-dependent	80 (88%)	10 (11%)	1 (1%)		
23. Primarily save the tax-payer money	13 (14%)	24 (26%)	17 (19%)	37 (41%)	
24. Assist women on welfare get jobs of their choice	56 (62%)	28 (30%)	6 (6%)	1 (1%)	1 (1%)
25. Force everyone to go to work	3 (3%)	5 (5%)	21 (23%)	60 (67%)	2 (2%)
26. Make welfare women work for their keep	6 (6%)	9 (10%)	22 (24%)	51 (57%)	3 (3%)
27. Help those who are able to move ahead in life	70 (77%)	17 (19%)	2 (2%)	2 (2%)	
28. Make the government look good	4 (4%)	9 (10%)	7 (19%)	61 (67%)	
29. Give welfare women the know-how of running their own lives	51 (56%)	33 (37%)	5 (5%)	2 (2%)	
30. Provide cheap labor for the big business	1 (1%)	3 (3%)	9 (10%)	77 (85%)	1 (1%)

TABLE 20

DROP-OUTS' PERCEPTION OF THE GOALS OF THE WIN PROGRAM

"As I understand it the WIN program was established in order to":

N=95

Items	Strongly agree	Somewhat agree	Somewhat disagree	Strongly disagree	No answer
21. Give women on welfare another chance in life	68 (72%)	20 (21%)	1 (1%)	3 (3%)	3 (3%)
22. Help welfare women become self-dependent	73 (77%)	13 (14%)	3 (3%)	1 (1%)	5 (5%)
23. Primarily save the tax-payer money	20 (21%)	20 (21%)	18 (19%)	28 (30%)	9 (9%)
24. Assist women on welfare get jobs of their choice	56 (59%)	30 (32%)	3 (3%)	2 (2%)	5 (4%)
25. Force everyone to go to work	9 (9%)	9 (9%)	18 (19%)	52 (56%)	7 (7%)
26. Make welfare women work for their keep	15 (16%)	23 (24%)	17 (18%)	31 (33%)	9 (9%)
27. Help those who are able to move ahead in life	70)74%)	18 (19%)		4 (4%)	3 (3%)
28. Make the government look good	7 (7%)	17 (18%)	23 (24%)	40 (43%)	8 (8%)
29. Give welfare women the know-how of running their own lives	53 (57%)	25 (26%)	5 (5%)	7 (7%)	5 (5%)
30. Provide cheap labor for the big business	9 (9%)	6 (6%)	14 (15%)	62 (66%)	4 (4%)

102

TABLE 21

STAFF'S PERCEPTION OF THE CLIMATE OF OPERATIONS OF THE WIN OFFICE

Staff N=21	Strongly agree	Somewhat agree	Somewhat disagree	Strongly disagree	No Answer
31. The WIN office was a really nice, friendly place	8 (38%)	12 (57%)	1 (5%)		
32. The WIN personnel treated the Enrollees as persons with special needs and interests	7 (33%)	14 (66%)			
33. One could say that the general philosophy of the office was that strict rules do not guarantee efficiency	6 (29%)	11 (52%)	3 (14%)	1 (5%)	
34. As the office was run, training was just one of the WIN experiences	5 (24%)	15 (71%)	1 (5%)		
35. People working there seemed relaxed doing their jobs	4 (19%)	16 (76%)	1 (5%)		
36. The consensus seemed to be that transportation to and from the WIN office was an important factor of the WIN program and therefore concerned Enrollees and staff alike	4 (19%)	12 (57%)	5 (24%)		
37. The primary concern of the WIN personnel was the general welfare of the Enrollee no matter what the consequences of the Enrollee's involvement with the program	5 (24%)	15 (71%)	1 (5%)		
38. The general procedure was to include the Enrollee's job interests in the selection of the employability plan	10 (48%)	11 (52%)			
39. The consensus seemed to be that day care arrangements were an important factor for the WIN program and therefore concerned Enrollees and staff alike	14 (16%)	7 (33%)			
40. The general philosophy was that primarily the WIN office was a social service agency rather than a training school	4 (19%)	10 48%	5 (24%)	2 (9%)	

103

TABLE 22

SUCCESSES' PERCEPTION OF THE CLIMATE OF OPERATIONS OF THE WIN OFFICE

Successes N=91	Strongly agree	Somewhat agree	Somewhat disagree	Strongly disagree	No answer
31. The WIN office was a really nice, friendly place	70 (77%)	17 (19%)	2 (2%)	1 (1%)	1 (1%)
32. The WIN personnel treated the Enrollees as persons with special needs and interests	68 (75%)	29 (22%)	2 (2%)	1 (1%)	
33. One could say that the general philosophy of the office was that strict rules do not guarantee efficiency	35 (39%)	34 (38%)	10 (11%)	8 (8%)	4 (4%)
34. As the office was run, training was just one of the WIN experiences	49 (55%)	20 (22%)	14 (15%)	5 (5%)	3 (3%)
35. People working there seemed relaxed doing their jobs	58 (65%)	24 (26%)	4 (4%)	3 (3%)	2 (2%)
36. The consensus seemed to be that transportation to and from the WIN office was an important factor of the WIN program and therefore concerned Enrollees and staff alike	63 (70%)	20 (22%)	5 (5%)	3 (3%)	
37. The primary concern of the WIN personnel was the general welfare of the Enrollee no matter what the consequences of the Enrollee's involvement with the program	47 (53%)	28 (30%)	11 (12%)	4 (4%)	1 (1%)
38. The general procedure was to include the Enrollee's job interests in the selection of the employability plan	64 (71%)	21 (23%)	3 (3%)	3 (3%)	
39. The consensus seemed to be that day care arrangements were an important factor for the WIN program and therefore concerned Enrollees and staff alike	68 (75%)	17 (19%)	4 (4%)	1 (1%)	1 (1%)
40. The general philosophy was that primarily the WIN office was a social service agency rather than a training school	35 (39%)	24 (26%)	18 (20%)	12 (13%)	2 (2%)

TABLE 23

DROP-OUTS' PERCEPTION OF THE CLIMATE OF OPERATIONS OF THE WIN OFFICE

Drop-Outs N=95	Strongly agree	Somewhat agree	Somewhat disagree	Strongly disagree	No answer
31. The WIN office was a really nice, friendly place	69 (73%)	18 (19%)	3 (3%)	3 (3%)	2 (2%)
32. The WIN personnel treated the Enrollees as persons with special needs and interests	62 (66%)	21 (22%)	5 (5%)	5 (5%)	2 (2%)
33. One could say that the general philosophy of the office was that strict rules do not guarantee efficiency	38 (40%)	25 (26%)	12 (13%)	14 (15%)	6 (6%)
34. As the office was run, training was just one of the WIN experiences	48 (51%)	20 (21%)	10 (10%)	12 (13%)	5 (5%)
35. People working there seemed relaxed doing their jobs	65 (69%)	21 (22%)	3 (3%)	2 (2%)	4 (4%)
36. The consensus seemed to be that transportation to and from the WIN office was an important factor of the WIN program and therefore concerned Enrollees and staff alike	59 (62%)	18 (19%)	12 (13%)	2 (2%)	4 (4%)
37. The primary concern of the WIN personnel was the general welfare of the Enrollee no matter what the consequences of the Enrollee's involvement with the program	45 (48%)	32 (34%)	8 (8%)	2 (2%)	8 (8%)
38. The general procedure was to include the Enrollee's job interests in the selection of the employability plan	50 (53%)	29 (31%)	6 (6%)	3 (3%)	7 (7%)
39. The consensus seemed to be that day care arrangements were an important factor for the WIN program and therefore concerned Enrollees and staff alike	64 (68%)	19 (20%)	1 (1%)	2 (2%)	9 (9%)
40. The general philosophy was that primarily the WIN office was a social service agency rather than a training school	34 (36%)	28 (30%)	8 (8%)	17 (18%)	8 (8%)

versus that of a social services agency. This last perspective supports the previous observation regarding the not-so-positive experiences "welfare" clients usually have with social welfare institutions.

5.   Statistical computations.   The testing of the hypotheses involved three sets of comparisons on each of the four variables. Specifically, it was hypothesized that there would be no significant differences between Staff and Successes while Drop-Outs would differ from both these groups.

While there are missing answers in all three population groups, a number of Drop-Outs indicated so few responses that they were considered unreliable. They were therefore excluded from the final computations. The basis for their exclusion was the enrollee's failure to respond to at least half of the questions in each area. A total of six (6) Drop-Outs were thus excluded.

The distribution characteristics of the scores on each relationship are given in Table 24 for each of the three study samples.

TABLE 24

MEANS AND STANDARD DEVIATIONS OF STAFF,
SUCCESSES AND DROP-OUTS FOR ALL
FOUR VARIABLES

| Population | | Experiences | Variables | | |
			Needs	Goals	Operations
Staff	M	34.381	30.762	33.952	32.095
N=22	SD	1.962	4.763	3.721	2.982
Successes	M	35.297	25.681	35.516	34.604
N=91	SD	4.070	7.476	4.127	5.138
Drop-Outs	M	33.281	25.101	33.461	33.921
N=89	SD	6.197	8.037	4.585	5.251

A quick view of this table confirms the analysis of the differences made earlier.

The multivariate analysis of variance comparing Staff
and Successes indicates an overall p value of .009.
This was not predicted by the hypotheses. Looking
closer into the Staff versus Successes comparison
(Table 25) through univariate tests, we see that the
difference is manifested in needs (p .0006) and operations (p .04) but not in experiences or goals. As
seen earlier, Successes score much lower in needs than
Staff, but higher on operations.

TABLE 25

RESULTS OF UNIVARIATE F TESTS FOR
STAFF VS SUCCESSES

Factor	Mean Sq.	
Experiences	14.309	p > .05
Needs	440.423	p < .05
Goals	41.742	p > .05
Operations	107.423	p < .05

The second comparison attempted was that of Staff
versus Drop-Outs. With an overall p value of .001 the
multivariate analysis of variance indicates that the
difference between the two groups is significant indeed. As seen in Table 25, however, univariate tests
indicate that the difference is manifested only in
needs (p .002).

TABLE 26

RESULTS OF UNIVARIATE F TESTS FOR
STAFF VS DROP-OUTS

Factor	Mean Sq.	
Experiences	20.561	p > .05
Needs	544.464	p < .05
Goals	4.108	p > .05
Operations	46.659	p > .05

The final comparison involves the two groups of enrollees. The multivariate analysis of variance comparing Successes and Drop-Outs indicates an overall p value of .014. A closer look into this comparison through univariate tests (Table 27) indicates that the difference is in experiences (p .012) and goals (p .001). On both these factors Successes score much higher than the Drop-Outs.

TABLE 27

RESULTS OF UNIVARIATE F TESTS FOR
SUCCESSES VS DROP-OUTS

Factor	Mean Sq.	
Experiences	162.396	$p < .05$
Needs	12.475	$p > .05$
Goals	191.694	$p < .05$
Operations	53.005	$p > .05$

To recapitulate, there were 12 hypotheses tested involving comparisons between Successes and Drop-Outs and between Staff and each of the enrollee groups, on four factors: experiences, needs, goals, and operations. The findings substantiated five of these hypotheses. The following is a synopsis of the relationships, the hypotheses made and the findings.

1. Staff - Successes

	Factor	Hypothesis	Findings
a.	Experiences	No difference	Confirmed
b.	Needs	No difference	Not confirmed
c.	Goals	No difference	Confirmed
d.	Operations	No difference	Not confirmed

2. Staff - Drop-Outs

	Factor	Hypothesis	Findings
a.	Experiences	Difference	Not confirmed
b.	Needs	Difference	Confirmed
c.	Goals	Difference	Not confirmed
d.	Operations	Difference	Not confirmed

3. Successes - Drop-Outs

	Factor	Hypothesis	Findings
a.	Experiences	Difference	Confirmed
b.	Needs	Difference	Not confirmed
c.	Goals	Difference	Confirmed
d.	Operations	Difference	Not confirmed

A very interesting finding is that there are indeed differences between Successes and Drop-Outs in their perception of the WIN experiences. However, as both of these groups agree with the Staff as to the nature of the supportive transactions, one may again want to assign this difference to the volume of experiences rather than their quality. The discussion in the following chapter gives credence to this interpretation. So do a number of other studies reviewed earlier.

It is difficult to carry the above argument to the interpretation of the differences found in goals. Again Successes and Drop-Outs disagree in their perceptions, while they both are in agreement with the Staff. A simple way of viewing this difference is to attribute it to a more enthusiastic Success group who, after all, "got what they wanted," so to speak. The same enthusiasm may count for their perception of the climate of the WIN office. One may stretch this point further and see the Drop-Outs' agreement on the style of WIN operations as supporting the earlier argument that both enrollees found WIN a positive program.

What seems more interesting, however, is the difference found between enrollees and staff in their perceptions of needs. As explained earlier in this work, this group of enrollees had undergone a battery of psychological tests, the result of which was known to the WIN staff. It seemed natural to assume that this staff would have as accurate an evaluation of what these enrollees needed as possible. Yet there is a significant difference in their perceptions.

The first temptation in interpreting the difference found in the perception of needs is to either question the validity of the psychological tests or that of this instrument or both. However, one may wish to probe further into the nature of the needs and the situational context of their evaluation. That is, one may include the component of the setting, that of a

109

manpower training program, and then see these needs as they relate to the objectives at hand. While the original psychological tests examined the "state-of-the-person" which the enrollee described, the present questionnaire asked the respondents to assess a need in relationship to training for employment, a qualified assessment. It is tempting thus to interpret the difference as stemming from a disparate perspective that the staff and enrollees had, rather than from poor diagnosis on the part of the former or denial on the part of the latter. The following discussion of the oral interviews provides supportive information which allows a better understanding of this point.

CHAPTER V

THE PARTICIPANTS SPEAK OUT

A more descriptive understanding of the experiences the WIN enrollees have while in training was sought through personal contacts with both enrollees and staff.

Since this part of the study was exploratory in nature, there was no specific theoretical point of departure. That is, although there was an identification of the enrollee as a Success or Dropout, no effort was made to secure that there would be the same set of questions posited in exactly the same manner, so to allow for accurate comparisons between the two groups and thus assess the hypotheses further. Nor was any effort made to structure the staff's responses so that both groups of enrollees were given equal time. The purpose of these interviews was simply to capture as closely as possible the actual interactions between staff and enrollees, to collect descriptive documentation of the nature of services offered, and to give an opportunity to those who were involved with the program to tell their side of the story. They were conducted in the hope that they would yield data which could assist us in furthering our understanding of the helping process and in identifying the situational context and service needs of people entering manpower programs.

The effort to trace enrollees provided a serendipitous third source of descriptive data, namely relatives and persons who worked with WIN enrollees and WIN staff. The latter include relatives of enrollees, hospital personnel officials, nursing directors, nurses in charge of hospital programs for nurses and nurses' aides, and officials of other training programs such as Maricopa County Skill Center and Arizona State Department of Vocational Rehabilitation.

The findings of these contacts are discussed separately for each group.

Enrollees

As stated in Chapter III, the questionnaire was mailed to all enrollees along with a letter explaining the purpose of the study and requesting their assistance.

Also through the letter the enrollees were asked whether there were other aspects of their WIN experience which they wished to communicate in a personal interview.

Of the eighty-two (82) enrollees who returned the questionnaire by mail, thirty-four (34) expressed interest in being interviewed. Six (6) enrollees included letters or written comments along with the questionnaire. One enrollee sent a written evaluation of the WIN program but no questionnaire.

Only six (6) of the enrollees who expressed interest in discussing their WIN experience further were interviewed. Approximately one third of them could not be reached at the time of the inquiry. As the majority of the responses to the questionnaire were secured through personal interviews, the descriptive data were sought at the time of the interviews. One hundred and four (104) enrollees were thus interviewed: fifty-four (54) of them Drop-Outs and fifty (50) Successes.

The usual approach of the interview was to ask the enrollee to expand on the questionnaire. That is, the enrollee was asked to clarify her answer by giving concrete descriptions or examples relevant to the statement in the question. The emphasis was on the first part of the questionnaire which deals with specific experiences the enrollee had with the WIN personnel. Enrollees volunteered comments on the other parts of the questionnaire as they responded to the questions. Notes of the responses were taken in the presence of the enrollees.

As the primary concern of this part of the study was to understand the actual exchanges between WIN enrollees and WIN staff, the enrollee was asked: "Mrs. A, you say that the WIN person assigned to you was deeply concerned that you become a happier person (or whatever the respondent's answer in the questionnaire was). What did he or she do to make you feel this way?" If the answers were dealing merely with feelings--for example "he was really nice" or "she really cared"--the enrollee was asked to clarify further with concrete examples. Most of the enrollees volunteered the information about how the WIN affected their lives and, although not all of them were equally eloquent in their descriptions, they seemed eager to talk about their WIN experience. It is worth noting that several enrollees volunteered to bring the interviewer in touch with other WIN women. Three enrollees even initiated the contact at the encouragement of their WIN friends who had already taken part in the study.

It must be clarified that no special attempt was made in these interviews to establish whether Successes maintained the original job they had obtained through WIN. There are two reasons for this omission. As the questionnaire did not include a request for this information, there was no way of establishing comparative data for all respondents. Secondly, the basic concern of the study is the role of supportive services in the enrollee's completing her employability plans, not the stability of her job or the level of wages she received. Such variables, as the review of the literature indicated, depend basically on labor market considerations. As stated earlier, the local standard of wages is usually low. Most importantly, though, these last years--and definitely the year of the investigation--were marked by high, nationwide unemployment. In Maricopa County unemployment reached more than 19.0% high. It would have been futile, therefore, to try to assess the employment potential of the Phoenix WIN office efforts at a time like this. Nevertheless, it was parenthetically ascertained that a great number of the enrollees maintained their original jobs, and a considerable number of Drop-Outs were now working. A number of the Successes were found to have even improved on their original jobs.

There seems to be no clear difference between Successes and Drop-Outs in their evaluation of their WIN experiences. There were only four respondents who were definitely and consistently negative about their WIN experience. They were equally divided between the two groups. Perhaps one Drop-Out was more emphatic in her comments than the three others. In her words, "All I carry are extremely bad memories and feelings about the entire experience. . . . The staff cared only for their coffee and salary. They never offered advice and support. Instead they were quick to criticize and undermine one's self-confidence." The other three enrollees commented on the need to have more options of training because "not all interests could be accommodated;" the staff's concern with bettering their own jobs rather than helping; and the boredom one experienced having to go through a routine which was not geared to the different needs of the enrollees.

Except for one Success who stated that she made it despite the WIN's limitations and one Drop-Out who

"simply got nothing" from the program, all other enrollees ascribed the limited results of their training
to their own particular conditions. This last group
includes two Successes who "settled" for a lesser
employability plan than the one suggested by the WIN
personnel. Both these women accepted their "own limitations." More specifically, one became a nurse's
aide because the planned practical nurse vocation
required more time for preparation than she "was willing to spend"; the other chose to be a "meat packer"
because the suggested job as electronics assembler was
more complicated than she "could tackle." Among the
Drop-Outs, reasons for failing included "when you got
problems at home you can't go to school, right?"; "I
was too young, I had no children, I couldn't get interested in the things the other women talked about";
"the pay wasn't enough"; "I wanted to be a police
woman. That was the only thing I wanted, but they
didn't let me"; "I tried to accept my own limitations
but I wasn't able." This last one wanted to train for
"barber-cosmetologist" but "the requirements changed"
and she "didn't want to put up with all the schooling."

The remaining responses were basically positive, leaving the clear impression that WIN was a very valuable
experience to them. If there is an "overall" difference in the responses of the two groups, perhaps it is
in the higher level of enthusiasm in the responses of
Successes. But then, the ones who stand out in their
descriptions are those Successes who have been able to
make significant changes in their lives, both financially and socially, through the WIN program. Their
enthusiasm may stem from their specific accomplishments, or it may be the result of the same personal
alertness that led to such accomplishments in the
first place. Therefore, as these differences are not
measurable, the enrollee's comments will be grouped in
the study areas they address, with indications as to
the status of the respondent when necessary.

1. Experiences. The overwhelming evidence from this
report is that the enrollees did indeed experience the
concern, care, and involvement of the WIN staff.
Their transactions were beneficial both because of the
quality of the people as well as the nature of the
services offered. The following discussion is organized around the characteristics that were identified
as helpful based on the descriptions of enrollees.

Examples of helpfulness mentioned most frequently by the enrollees are given along with statements of feelings. Specific vignettes are given at the end of the discussion for those items which require further description of characteristic transactions.

With the exception of two qualified answers* for most of the enrollees "the people in the WIN made all the difference." This difference was made through the staff's:

Support: "People in the WIN were behind me all the way." "They supported me in all the hassles that others gave me." "They will call and keep in touch with me even when I was skipping classes." "When one got a job everyone was so proud!" "They would come to graduation and celebrate with you." "They never made you feel bad. If it doesn't work, we'll try again."

Examples cited: WIN personnel often visited skill labs, schools, hospitals where enrollees were training and talked with teachers, trying to iron out difficulties and find ways of assisting. They arranged for purchase of uniforms or other appropriate clothing, so that enrollees would not be delayed in their job placement when jobs were found unexpectedly. They supported the college attendance of enrollees (two such instances) while enrollees were recorded on "hold" component.

Availability: "They tried to help you beyond their own jobs." "Always had time to answer your questions." "I had always someone available to help me." "They were there any time you needed them for anything you needed."

Examples cited: WIN personnel gave the enrollees their home phone numbers so that the enrollees could reach them any time. Babysat for children if needed. Organized dinners and parties for evenings and weekends for those enrollees who were lonely. Volunteered transportations for doctors' visits, shopping, and other such needed activities.

_____

*The two separate statements are: "Just one lady was not supportive but all the others were helpful" and "Some were not so good but the majority were really nice people."

Provision of Models: "Many knew how it was like and wanted to help." "She was on welfare before, had problems with her husband and things like that, and now she has all these degrees. She is an inspiration to people, I guess." "They told you they have done as many shitty things as you did." "This lady admitted she had an illegitimate son. She made me feel I was not the only dummy in the world." "When that blind worker told her story, I saw others were worse off than us. She made it. I told myself I can make it, too."

Examples cited: WIN personnel will often discuss their own life experiences and ways of coping. There would be regular sessions when WIN graduates were brought to discuss their own stories and the ways to their success.

Knowledge and Reliability: "She knew her job." "She was not one of those fly-by-night." "Was not a repeat. She could cope with any situation." "Tried to help you as best as they could. If they couldn't, they tried to suggest what would make you happy." "They tried to find out what you want to do, what you are capable of doing, to help you to go through."

Examples cited: WIN personnel assisted the enrollees in securing health and dental care, purchasing of glasses, clothes, and other necessary items. They were able to secure funds for RN and college training. They intervened on behalf of their clients for food stamps, commodity goods, and so on. They established contacts with other training programs, testing facilities, and other auxiliary services.

Personal Involvement: "Your future meant a lot to them." "The way they showed interest in you . . . tried to explain to you . . . I just learned a whole lot." "It was a whole family experience. They wanted the kids to know mother would not be there to watch them and somebody else will be with them."

Examples cited: Commodity goods were shared and pot luck dinners were prepared by enrollees and staff. Evenings and weekend activities were arranged for all, often at the homes of WIN staff members. WIN personnel collected newspapers for recycling so to secure petty cash for clients' emergencies.

Enthusiasm: "She herself had so much confidence in herself that overflowed in you."   "You gained confidence just talking to them."   "That attitude! Like nothing can stop you."   "Had a smile on their faces every day."   "They were telling you never to give up." "Made you feel you are never too old to start."   "They dared me do things."

Examples cited: Often enrollees were encouraged to follow a career line, as for instance start with nurse's aide and continue to practical and registered nursing.   Many enrollees commented on their present status as being the direct result of their having been "challenged for more" or been "taught to always try for more."

Trust in and Respect for the Enrollees: "Made you feel you are not an outcast."   "They tried to make us see better aspects of our life."   "Like just because you are on welfare that does not mean you are nothing."   "Made us feel we are entitled to the money." "Don't go around with you head hanging down."   "They told me what were my weak points and how my strong points could make it."

Examples cited: The sharing of many activities was seen by the employees as an indication of trust and a sense of being equal.   Said an enrollee about the common dinners prepared by enrollee, from commodity goods: "They were not afraid to eat.   We were as clean as they were."   "Mother's hats," an around the room discussion about how many hats a mother wears: a cook, a friend, nurse, playmate, and so on.   Said a young enrollee: "It made me feel so important because I was all these things to my baby."

Besides the above discussed general experiences, there are certain items whose probing gave some interesting, individualized transactions.   A selection of these transactions follows:

Item 5:   The enrollee is asked what would the worker do in times of trouble.   The most positive answer is that the WIN worker was sympathetic and suggested practical solutions.   Some such solutions:

- When an enrollee received a traffic ticket, the worker accompanied her to the court hearing.   Says the enrollee: "I was so scared but she helped me survive the experience."

117

- WIN worker interceded with the landlord when one enrollee was late in rent payment because of delay in receiving her ADC monthly check.

- WIN manager put her own stocks on collateral to prevent repossession of an enrollee's refrigerator when the latter was late in making her payments.

- WIN worker arranged with city bus driver to delay at a certain bus stop so an enrollee passenger could take her child to the nursery and return to catch the same bus, thus saving the mother both money and time.

- When an enrollee was unhappy about the child care arrangements, WIN worker helped her find another center near the WIN office so not to have complications of transportation.

Item 6: This is a hypothetical situation where the enrollee has car trouble and cannot go to the WIN office. The most positive answer is that the WIN worker helps the enrollee make such arrangements that she was no longer faced with this difficulty.

- Worker picked up enrollee and towed her car to Maricopa Technical College for repairs. This was an often mentioned incident. Such repairs were made for free, as the students used the cars for their own training.

- WIN arranged with LEAP (Leadership Education for the Advancement of Phoenix) an inner city self-support organizational credit union for a loan so that enrollee could purchase a car. This example was also often cited.

Item 7: This is another hypothetical situation. The enrollee is presented with a serious personal difficulty, a grave family problem, which upsets her to the point that she cannot do well in her training. The most positive answer is that the WIN worker will make it possible for her to continue her training while helping her handle her problem.

- An enrollee's little girl was in a serious car accident and was hospitalized. WIN staff members donated blood and took turns staying with the child who was in intensive care. In this way, the mother

118

was able to continue her schooling feeling confident that someone was always with the little girl.

- Another case of illness of a child. The WIN worker interceded and rearranged the mother's school schedule so she could stay with her child longer hours during the day.

- After a violent attack by her ex-husband, an enrollee was so frightened that she could not stay in her apartment. WIN staff members found her other lodgings and moved her belongings by themselves in a worker's pickup van.

It is interesting that purely training activities are not among the experiences reported as "helpful" by the enrollees. Of course, the questionnaire did not gear to them; nevertheless, the discussions were open-ended enough for the enrollee to wander in that direction if she wished to. The closest the responses came to training--relating helpful transactions--were in Item 9 where the enrollees were asked what would the WIN worker do if something in the way an enrollee looked or behaved could interfere with her preparing for a job. Examples given with appreciation are simulated office interviews, role playing, films on how to dress, walk, meet people, or even visits by various employers who explained what they want or do not want from an employee. Even then, though, the instances of helpful transactions most frequently mentioned were those removing barriers rather than developing skills.

2. Needs. Contrary to the results of the questionnaire, the responses to the interview left no doubt that the enrollees felt that they entered the WIN program with many personal needs, and it was the meeting of these needs that was the first benefit of their WIN experience. Although there was some acknowledgement of all of the needs referred to in the questionnaire, the overwhelming majority of the interviewed women talked primarily about their lack of confidence and social shyness. For instance, only six women commented specifically about their difficulties in handling their children prior to entering WIN. As one put it, "I used to be a screaming mother. I felt I should have to hurt my kids physically in order to punish them. Now I have learned to put limits and have fun with them." Many, however, commented appreciatively about the films and other "how-to" demonstrations which gave them clues regarding better mothering. Said one young mother: "I had never been

119

around children to know what to do with my baby." Two
ladies volunteered descriptions of their previously
uncontrollable temper. One emphasized that "even my
mother couldn't do anything about it." She was quite
proud of the way she was now able to handle her anger
and "not just get mad." Very few were the expressions
of the need to budget time and money. Regarding
money, many actually commented that "there wasn't any
money to budget anyhow." But, again, there was strong
appreciation expressed for the tips given to them
about how to schedule their activities so to allow for
fun, or for the recipes given to them for low-cost
cooking and other such house-managing aides.

In a way many of these responses could be considered
contradictory, as there was no explicit admission of
need, yet there was an implicit admission in the enrollees' acknowledgment of benefit. However, such an
acknowledgment may also be seen as the enrollee's
ability to improve her previous skills with the utilization of new knowledge. Then there is the other
perspective expressed by many enrollees, that one does
not know what one is missing until the time one real-
izes that its attainment is possible. As one young
Success put it, "When I entered the WIN I didn't think
I needed anything, but as I moved on I saw the benefit
of the experience. I came to appreciate the social
services."

One need that nobody denied was that for building
self-confidence. In one way or another all the interviewed women stated that they entered WIN with a very
low profile. As a matter of fact it was made clear
that it was because of the WIN experience that they
were able to talk to the interviewer. Some examples
of the before-and-after state: "I used to feel
ashamed and shy. I was really down on myself. Now I
am willing to take chances." "Before, I would say
'Why should I go? I will fail.' Now I go whether I
flunk or not." "I felt I was the lowest one. There I
saw I was like lots of others. That couldn't be so
bad." "Before, I couldn't go any place, take the bus,
talk to people. I feel stronger as a person after the
WIN experience." "I was as low emotionally as you can
get. WIN made me feel human and worthwhile. Like
there is a place in life for you." "I have learned
that I am just as good as everybody else. Never had
that before." "I went in as a second class citizen.
Came out number one. WIN made us better persons. We
were such a bunch of mistreated women, you know!"

The last comment is representative of what the enrollees offered as the reason for their lack of
confidence. Many discussed that there was such a fear
in "The idea of getting out and seeing what was going
on in the world. Hell, there was not enough money to
even afford a magazine to see what is going on in the
world." "I had not worked for a long time. I had
been home for years with a sick daughter. I wasn't
seeing anybody. Well, you know, I would see the land-
lady when I paid the rent or the grocer when I bought
groceries. . . ." "When you have been told you are
dumb for so long, you don't find you can do many
things." "It is debilitating to be on welfare. I was
just home looking and retarding." "Being out of
school for eighteen years, being on welfare, with
kids, at my age and being divorced--I needed someone
to convince me I can do it and help me with it." "I
was bitter. I had been kicked in the mouth so often.
I was angry. Hard to keep my temper when I was forced
to put my face down so many times. It is hard to be
on welfare. Degrading!" "The traumatic experiences
welfare women go through--you know, you keep yourself
like in a shell. Just going out and not being afraid!
. . ."

"Out" is the world beyond the familiar. In the words
of one enrollee echoing many others, "I was not afraid
to work, but I was not prepared." Surprisingly, the
description of "not prepared" had very little to do
with training or possession of skills. Most of the
women talked in terms of personal readiness and direction. "They give you all those lab tests and aptitude
tests. You find out a lot about yourself . . . you
never thought you could do it." "When I went there I
didn't know what I wanted to be. I needed someone to
tell me what is what, to help me make a decision." "I
went through tests, discussion, just to find out what
I can do and what is around." "I had never worked
before. I was terrified I will not find my way back
home." "When I went there I didn't even know how to
take a bus. Now I know how to drive. I can go
around." "I used to talk to no one. Now I can talk
to anyone I want to. They showed me how to confront
people, how to ask for things." "I used to be so shy.
I never could talk to anyone before. Now I stand up
for my right too. . . ." "I have a better vocabulary
now. I can communicate now even if I don't use all of
the new words I learned." "I used to feel so ashamed
and shy. I didn't know how to read real good. Now I
have my GED!" "I was shy and could never speak. I
have changed. I try to do things for myself." "I

came out of my self-neglect. I get to places now, restaurants, museums, movies. Not just locked in my house as I was."

3. Goals. Whatever comments were made regarding the goals of the WIN program, they were reactions to the statements in the questionnaire. The statement that seemed to be most provocative was Item 30 which suggests that WIN was established in order to provide cheap labor for big business. "Oh no!" was the most frequent response with qualifications such as "They trained us for electronics, it means good money, right?" or "That is what I am getting now." Interestingly enough, both mentioned examples are statements of Drop-Outs, the latter from one who was in farm labor at the time of the interview.

Although there seemed to be considerable agreement that saving the taxpayer money (Item 23) was one of the goals of the WIN program, there was no corresponding agreement that WIN was aiming to force everyone to go to work, especially the welfare women (Items 25 and 26). Practically all enrollees stated that force was not what they experienced at the WIN. Some examples of the responses: "I was never pushed into anything." "They never pushed us in the job if we were unhappy." "They will not force you but try to help you to see how important it is." "They kind of stayed on you to go on with the program, but they did not force." "They did not want you to drop-out."

Item 29, dealing with the aim to give welfare women the know-how of running their own lives, brought a mixed response. The overall conclusion was that "some welfare women do need this assistance, some don't." On the other hand, there was emphatic support of Item 27 which suggests that the goal of the WIN is to help those who are able to move ahead in life. This "moving ahead" was seen not only in terms of moving financially--"gave you a steady job, not just little jobs here and there"--but mostly in terms of developing as a person. Some examples of the latter: "I got enough confidence from the experience." "Jobs are hard to find these days, you know. But they give you enough initiative to go out on your own when the job market and personal matters are O.K." And, to quote one Drop-Out, "not only those able. Everybody moved ahead in life."

There was considerable disagreement regarding the goal of assisting an enrollee get a job of her choice (Item 24). While a great number agreed that this was true, several enrollees pointed out that they could not get what they wanted because "not all interests could be accommodated." Both Successes and Drop-Outs commented on the fact that there were practically three lines of training: nursing, clerical, and some kind of computer work. The limitations of vocational opportunities were often given as the reason for dropping-out of the program.

Described as a "very important program," "fantastic" and "beautiful," WIN was seen in general as having the welfare of the recipient as its overall goal, at least at the level of its implementation. "Everyone was concerned about the person rather than get her off the government payroll." "They didn't even emphasize the financial." Item 28 provoked the enrollees' mirth with its suggestion that WIN was established in order to make the government look good. "It makes us look good, not the government!" The message communicated was that there was no pro-government advertisement in the implementation of the program and that there is no way that the government "can look good." As one Success wrote, "Win is the only redeeming feature in Arizona welfare."

4. <u>Operations</u>. Many of the statements already reported apply also to the ways the Phoenix WIN office was operating. For instance Items 36 and 39, referring to WIN's sharing in the responsibility for transportation and day-care arrangements did not present obstacles to an enrollee's training. In terms of transportation, car pools were organized, bus schedules were distributed, assistance for the repairing and purchasing of cars was offered, transportation was often directly provided, parking facilities were secured, and even interceding with the city's bus drivers for little favors and special accommodations was attempted. In terms of child care, information on day-care centers was secured, advocacy for licensing of convenient nurseries and day-care centers was exercised, and direct intervention with day-care facilities for the accommodation of enrollees was made. An interesting example of the latter, not yet discussed, is the arrangement that the WIN management made with a day-care center: The WIN personnel would advertise the center in exchange for the center's picking up the enrollees' children from the WIN office in the morning and returning them there in the afternoon. Thus an enrollee would have to plan only for one trip a day.

There was also consensus that the WIN office was a friendly place where people seemed enjoying doing their job (Items 31 and 35). In such an atmosphere, there was "liberal interpretation of rules" and a "relaxed pace," fitting "the individualized needs" of each enrollee.

Item 34, indicating that as the Phoenix WIN office was run, training was just one of the WIN experiences, received a strong endorsement by Successes and Drop-Outs alike. "You learned so much more than skills," was an often heard comment. Interestingly enough, in response to the same item, there were reactions such as "we had sessions regarding how to dress . . . how to meet people, role playing," which were not considered to be directly relating to skill development. An alert Success described such demonstrations as "preventive assistance" which, she emphasized, "was given" in a proper way, not "personalized," so one did not have to feel "singled out."

Item 38, which deals with the inclusion of the enrollee's job interests in the selection of employability plans, brought diverse responses. While there were agreeing statements like, "Look, I was good in math, so it was suggested I should go for electronics, but I was not happy with the idea, so they let me become a nurse," or "They would let you switch if you were unhappy"; there were also the previously reported statements that not all interests could be accommodated; there were even some angry ones that enrollees' interests were ignored. An example of the latter is the lady who wanted to be a police woman but who was not allowed to follow such a career. As it was reported before, this enrollee dropped out very frustrated and she has not worked since then. Another example was the young mother who wanted to become a nurse but was not found "suitable" for this line of work. Very angry, she dropped out of WIN and, in her words, "I went on my own." At the time of the interview she stated that she was attending practical nurses' training.

There was overall agreement that the primary concern of the WIN personnel was the general welfare of the enrollees, even if that meant that the enrollee should drop out of the program. Evidence of this agreement has already been given in the previous discussion. The impression of the enrollees was that "they didn't just try to shove you" and that "they will let you take off and give you the chance to try again" at a later time.

Perhaps the most controversial of all variables is Item 40 which describes the Phoenix office as primarily a social service agency rather than a training school. While there were a great number of enrollees--both Successes and Drop-Outs--who readily said, "that's what it was," many others protested such a comparison. The message in these protests was that WIN was "a beautiful program" in clear contrast to social service agencies. Yet there was a third kind of response--albeit minimal in volume--that expressed disagreement with the posited statement. Thus it is difficult to make an accurate analysis of this item.

Besides the responses directly related to the questionnaire, many enrollees offered overall impressions of their WIN experiences. Both Successes and Drop-Outs found that they still draw on those experiences. "WIN still has its effects on me." "Fantastic program! It helps you in ways you can use it in the future," said an enthusiastic young Success. Many of these "ways" have to do with how one manages one's affairs, how to handle everyday necessities. One, a Drop-Out, even commented on the credentials that her WIN participation has bestowed on her. "I have my WIN attendance card. It is very useful to me when I apply for a job."

Yet most women talked about the way WIN has affected them as persons in their self-image and outlook for life. Some examples: "Biggest change in developing competence. In a few days they could do it!" "I came to the WIN because welfare told me to. I had such a self-defeatist attitude. Look at me now." "They made me look for the future." "I had such hard experiences from welfare. Now I can do things." "Even the ones who did not succeed went away with a little more than what they had." "All should have the opportunity I had!" "Regardless of training or job we benefited." "I was encouraged to start life again. At my age!" "WIN gave me not just a job but a life."

This last statement, so often repeated, seems to sum the general impression of what most of these enrollees concluded to be the purpose of the WIN program: "Training is not just what matters." Some even went further and defined "success" in the program. For these women success is "not a job but to prepare you to find a job on your own." "To get you ready for one

125

[job], not to find you one." "Got confidence to look for a job when I was ready to work." "If you depend only on WIN to find you a job, then WIN fails in what they try to do." And, to quote a most articulate lady who, in her late forties and with a retarded child at home, became a police service clerk and is now working for a Bachelor degree in Social Work, "anything that gets an individual to be his own decision maker is success. Otherwise WIN is a failure."

Many recognized that the seed was in them and that the WIN experience gave it the opportunity to grow. "They were very good if you tried to cope." "It seemed everyone was on our side if we wanted to make it." "You must have some guts to go. But they helped open all the doors needed to become self-reliant." Or, as another successful nurse put it, "It was in me but they brought it out. They gave it a push. I got through WIN as far as I could go, then continued on my own."

The instillment of this "attitude" of the WIN is what many enrollees found "fantastic." The attitude that "although EPCed (Employability Plan Completed), this is not necessarily satisfactory. One should continually grow and look for more." As a Drop-Out said, "WIN put a backbone in us." And, in what can be seen as a different kind of proof of this looking-into-the-future attitude, a lady, for whom the special job of transportation aide* was created in a hospital, said with eyes shining with hope: "My daughter is going to WIN now!"

Staff

The contact with the Staff was even less structured than that with the enrollees. The specific effort of this contact was to understand the philosophical orientation and institutional context of service

---

*This case is a very interesting example of community cooperation. This certain lady wanted to be a nurse's aide but extreme limitations in managing English reading and writing made it impossible. Yet she was found to be so willing to apply herself that she was assigned the special duties of wheeling patients to and from laboratories for X rays or other tests or accompanying them for walks in the hospital's court yard.

delivery. No effort was made to secure specific examples of services rendered, as these were emphasized in the perspective of the client. Besides, it was felt that an _ex post facto_ inquiry could not lead to accurate identification of each enrollee by the worker and individualized assessment of the work done on her behalf. Nevertheless, examples were used by the staff members, and it was ascertained that several of these examples were the same ones described by the clients.

The input of the staff was secured in individual interviews and group meetings. While the emphasis of the information, and its lucidity, varied from worker to worker, the main points are as follows:

1. _Experiences._ The impression is that supportive services were seen by the WIN staff as the backbone of the service activity of the WIN program. Such services were described as a great array of resources and interventions which can benefit the enrollee. Examples of such interventions were: advocacy on behalf of the client to "welfare" and other "authority" institutions for the clients' rights. For instance, the WIN office negotiated with the Department of Economic Security to appoint a "welfare" worker at the WIN office so that the enrollees have easy access to welfare services. When the assigned person proved to be unsympathetic to the needs of the enrollees, the WIN staff again interceded and brought about his removal and replacement with a more sympathetic person. Examples of the staff's interference for the licensing of a nursery and accommodations by a day-care center have already been mentioned. The staff also saw themselves in the role of a "buffer," neutralizing or lessening the negative effects of societal pressures on the client. See, for instance, the examples of staff interceding with landlords, creditors, and so on already discussed by the enrollees. Public relations efforts on behalf of the client were also part of their responsibilities. Such efforts include contacts with prospective and actual employers, meetings with teachers, trainers, and other social agencies' officials.

Although the overall formula of direct service provision had the vague old-time recipe of "as-much-as-it-takes" quality, the emphasis was clearly on providing counseling with personal needs and concrete, day-to-day problems. Versatile in its form, as already seen, this emphasis allowed for two consequences. First, counselors were the ones to set the tone in the decisions of the team. What an enrollee needed was analyzed, as was the direction and pace of her training, in terms of personality components. Thus not only a "sympathetic" and "rehabilitative" approach prevailed, but recognition was given to expertise and value of knowledge. Secondly, for counseling to be effective, mobilization of community resources and utilization of all possible provision made by the program was seen as necessary. Thus systematic efforts were made to identify the resources and communicate the means of this manipulation. For instance regular staff meetings were scheduled in order to discuss the directives of the policy, to exchange information regarding what is available, and to share experiences of what has been tried and found successful. Such sessions included brainstorming on interpretation of policy and alternative approaches. The aim was seen as the development of knowledge and improvement of service.

There were also staff meetings of the encounter quality, where members examined their relationship to each other and their own personal needs and predicaments. The aim was to develop personal supports and easing of interpersonal exchanges.

Outside consultants were often called in order to facilitate both of the above processes. Also there was an interest in attending conferences, workshops, and other professional activities which could improve the serving capacity of the WIN personnel. A number of employees pursued professional careers or increased their professional credentials while at WIN.

2. Needs. Although often recognized as "maternal" and "overprotective," the staff's interest in WIN enrollees was seen as necessary because of the personal needs of the enrollees. Even in their most conservative evaluations, the WIN personnel found the enrollees needing in a variety of emotional and social areas. For instance when discussing this part of the questionnaire, no staff member indicated that perhaps some enrollees have some of the reported needs while some may not--a position clearly stated by the enrollees. On the contrary the staff indicated that the degree of each need varied but its presence was undisputed. It was even suggested that that section of the questionnaire should be given indicators of degree-- i.e., 1, 2, 3, 4, 5--rather than of the agree/disagree type.

128

3. <u>Goals</u>. Perhaps the above assumption was based on the fact that there was no scrutinizing admission requirements. Except for "obvious," "serious," and "current" physical illness, there were no objective criteria for screening enrollees. The goals of the WIN program were interpreted in the very general sense of benefiting a disadvantaged client in preparing for employment. The staff's attitude was that "everyone who wants to try should be given a chance," and, therefore, they were willing to accept anyone who showed interest in the program. Such willingness allowed for the staff's identification with the goals of the enrollee and even with the enrollee herself. See, for instance, the practice of utilizing themselves as examples, a practice so admired by the enrollees.

4. <u>Operations</u>. While identification with the client stimulated the worker's perseverance and determination to be of help, it did not allow, it was admitted, energy and time to accommodate all clients alike. Thus, not all enrollees were "active" cases. There was no formula offered of a "deserving" client or how choices were made on priorities of service. Nor was there any effort to organize the activity in ways that permit systematic appraisals of inputs and outcomes. The limited consideration for organizational matters was accompanied by a total lack of inhibition in the utilization of any available loophole in the program's policy and provision. Characteristic examples of this attitude was the earlier mentioned cases of enrollees who were attending college while reported on the "hold" component. College attendance was not within the provisions of the WIN training. Yet a "hold" designation was legitimate and allowed for three ambitious enrollees of this study's sample to pursue career interests and significantly improve their social and personal predicaments.

Whether such an optimum work atmosphere was the result of institutional promotion or a convergence of individual attitudes is hard to conclude. The activities of the workers had administrative sanction and their professional endeavors were administratively encouraged and facilitated. At the same time, a great number of the WIN employees were people who themselves had experienced hard times and were victorious over their own life obstacles. Perhaps, as is usually the case, there is a combination of factors that brought about the kind of enthusiasm and purpose to the discharge of professional functions that was found in the

Phoenix WIN office. As a result of the above, or
perhaps the very cause of it, there was a total involvement of the worker in the life of the enrollee.
This involvement was what most of the staff gave as
the basic principle of their practice.

Others

The contact with parties outside the study population
was unintentional. It came as a result of the effort
to locate enrollees at their homes and places of employment. Its value lies in the support of the data
already collected rather than the provision of new
information.

While most of the relatives commented on the specific
changes they saw in the person and life of the en-
rollee--i.e., "she was really happy," "she is more
outgoing now," "she made lots of friends there"--those
who worked with them dealt mostly with the efforts
made by the WIN staff. Such efforts included: better
social preparation (than other training programs);
frequent visits before and during training; follow-up
contacts after enrollee was placed on the job; flexibility and alertness as to potential problems' and
available opportunities. With regards to the latter,
employers commented that "although there was quite a
pressure to take in WIN women, when there was trouble
they [WIN staff] were willing to pull back. So when a
new job was possible, we called them again."

It is interesting that one of the complaints voiced
was that "there should be closer screening," as not
all of the enrollees were "ready" for employment when
placed. Yet, one person who expressed the above com-
plaint also commented: "I really admire them [the WIN
staff] because they rarely gave up on them [enroll-
ees]. They process them through two or three times,
and even after they quit and come back . . . I often
get angry because I think it is a waste of the taxpayer's money. But, you know, many of these women make
it the second time!"

CHAPTER VI

MAINSTREAMING: FREEING THE HUMAN POTENTIAL

The analysis of the findings of the questionnaire has
substantiated five of the twelve hypotheses, pointing
out relevant differences between Successes and Drop-
Outs in their perceptions of the WIN experiences, and
between Enrollees and Staff in their appraisal of
needs an enrollee has when entering the program.
There may be arguments raised as to whether the hypotheses were properly stated in the first place.
Nevertheless, the data collected in this study were
supported by findings elsewhere, thus allowing some
confidence as to the validity of the outcome.   For
instance, Audrey Smith and her associates found in
their follow-up of WIN women that these women were
very appreciative of having had the WIN opportunity,
and thought it was a major influence in improving many
aspects of their lives.[1]   Georgina Smith, as seen,
found that the enrollees' feelings were positive even
when work was not secured.[2]   So did Thompson and
Miles.[3]   Respondents in the Opton study found little
to criticize in the WIN program even though their
actual job placement benefits from it were not better
than from the state employment office, ". . . an agency towards which many were quite bitter and angry.
The difference in attitudes," concludes Opton, "may
result from different standards of interpersonal behavior the two programs instill in their staff."[4]   The
positive overall impressions of the enrollees with the
WIN staff explain the lack of any observable difference between Successes and Drop-Outs in the oral
interviews, when their experiences with WIN staff were
described.

Still the question remains why the statistical difference between Successes and Drop-Outs in their
perception of experiences and goals.   Again, at the
simplest level this difference may be understood as
reflecting the Drop-Outs' reaction to their having
"failed" to find a job.   Yet, should this explanation
be valid, the responses of Drop-Outs should have been
negative rather than, let us say, less enthusiastic.
And they should be at odds with the responses of the
Staff.   Furthermore, if having a job was the reason
for the satisfaction, shouldn't the Successes who were
unemployed at the time of the interview feel the
frustration with the futility of it all?   These
findings, too, agree with those of other studies.

Mangum and Robson, for instance, found that seven out of ten respondents felt positive about the training they had received, with those who had completed their training significantly more likely to have positive feelings than those who had not. However, the authors point out, "there was no consistent relationship between those expressions and the extent of improvement in wages or employment stability."[5] The interviews with the enrollees in the present study support this point, as most of the women described the change that the WIN experience affected on them in terms of a better self-image and a personal revitalization rather than in monetary improvements.

As, therefore, the range of services received by the two enrollee groups seem to have been the same, what distinguishes the Successes from the Drop-Outs is the former's longer exposure to them. As seen in a previous chapter, the average length of time for the Successes was 52 weeks, while the average for the Drop-Outs was less than 27 weeks. Or, to put it more dramatically, the average Success stayed in the WIN program twice as long as the average Drop-Out. Can this difference in stay account for the difference in the evaluation of the experience?

This interpretation is vulnerable. It does seem somewhat circular to say that the Successes received more of a good thing, thus they found it better. But then, significant though it was, the difference between the Successes' and Drop-Outs' evaluation of the WIN experience was one of degree rather than of quality. As stated earlier, the Successes did enjoy the accelerated benefits of a sustained, enabling experience. And enablement is how they described the opportunity they were given; namely, the structure and wherewithal to explore their capacities and affirm their identities. As educators and pedagogues have established, positive learning breeds positive learning; that is, the sense of accomplishment and confidence that the learner acquires, by moving successfully through a planned course of experience, paves[6] the way to more confidence and more accomplishment. On the other hand, the Drop-Outs, by leaving the program earlier, did not receive as full a benefit from their WIN experience.

The above discussion does not, of course, answer why the Drop-Outs left the program earlier. There are a number of factors which, considered synergistically, could partly explain the difference in the outcome. For instance, dropping-out of the program may be seen as reflecting the demographic character of that sample: younger women, more high school graduates and Blacks, with less dependents. Nationwide findings indicate that such characteristics seem to be associated with higher drop-out rates from training programs. The trend is related to a factor not considered in this study. Beginning in the antipoverty period of the sixties, many young minority high school graduates appear to reject various types of "dead-end" jobs, "dirty" work, domestic work, and the like, and are demanding jobs that are meaningful and have the possibility for advancement. WIN is very limited in the offers it can make, offers that can be easily refused. Yet, as far as this study is concerned, this is only a peripheral reason--if at all--as the demographics of the two populations show no significant difference.

Even more puzzling is the difference found between Staff and Enrollees in their assessment of the needs the enrollees have when entering the WIN program. This is the one factor on which both groups of Enrollees differ significantly from the Staff, while they reach almost absolute congruence among themselves. But then, as seen in the analysis of findings, the enrollees' response to the oral interviews qualified drastically the disparity in the Staff-Enrollee assessment. During these interviews, the enrollees left no doubt that they entered the WIN program with many personal needs. The meeting of these needs was what most of the enrollees considered the primary benefit of their WIN experience. Perhaps it should be repeated here that both the statistical findings and the verbal responses of the enrollees indicated the enrollees' objection to their being considered "inadequate" as far as their immediate environment was concerned but saw themselves handicapped in relationship to the "outside" world. This stand was again asserted in the discussion of the goals of the WIN program where "giving welfare women the know-how of running their own lives"--a positively meant goal--received only a hesitant endorsement, even after clarifications as to the intent of the question.

The question of who assesses the problem more accurately, the client or the helping professional, has long been an issue of controversy in professional dialogue, leading to separation of financial assistance from social services, to the client-as-a-consumer movements, even to the mythification of mental illness. Yet, "a problem," Robert Perlman

133

says, "is the outcome of an act of definition on the part of an individual,"[8] a relational concept. When defined by the client, the profile of a presenting problem is very much culturally and ideologically determined. This does not mean that people of the same demographics necessarily behave alike in their encounters with social agencies. Differences in the ways that people perceive and act on their troubles are traceable to the disparate conditions they experience because of their sociodemographic characteristics as well as to less tangible variables--their values, beliefs, life-styles, aspirations, and expectations from themselves and the world around them. Howard, and his colleagues, for instance, in their work with the disabled, found that the rate of self-defined disability is higher when socioeconomic conditions indicate a more restricted opportunity structure for employment[9] and is lower when these conditions are more favorable.

On the other hand, the definition of a client's problem by the helping professional includes some interpretation of the relationship of the problem to the solution sought, that is, an evaluation--diagnosis, if you will--of the presenting situation along with what is needed for the desired, planned change. To quote Perlman again, "even in the verbatim statement . . . the recording of people's problems inevitably involves judgments on the part of workers and some transposition of the material into prescriptive terms."[10] Thus the helping professional evaluates the needs of the client in her/his relationship to the service goals. While this goal was understood by the WIN enrollee in terms of employment, for the worker it had the broader meaning of becoming ready for employment. And here is, perhaps, where the crucial point lies. The services developed seemed to have been based on an evaluated social disability of the client and were aimed at eliminating precisely that, at least as a first step to training. The clients seemed not to allow for themselves the luxury of enablement. These women, burdened by the social criticisms of the welfare clients, and themselves sharing these societal beliefs, ascribed to the needs value characteristics instead of recognizing them as practical concomitants to training. Yet, the fact that they found the services they received satisfactory and beneficial implies the accuracy of the staff's perception, or at least indicates some validity in the staff's evaluation of the clients' needs.

Existential Emphraxis

We may therefore draw the first conclusion from the findings of this study. Despite concepts[11] of "culture of poverty" or "disreputable poverty,"[11] and their implication of a subculture of the welfare poor, the value orientations of the women enrolling in the WIN program stem from the larger American culture rather than from their particular demographic subgroup. That is, the average WIN mother wishes for herself the same kind of life that any woman anywhere in Middle-America does. To suggest that the women on welfare have substituted a revered ethic with one of questionable virtue implies that these women enjoy their situation, that they have dynamically sought its attainment and thus now are fulfilled and gratified. Yet it has been demonstrated that the welfare status quo is not a cherished one and that membership in it seems to be unavoidable rather than welcome. Its apparent acceptance should be seen, therefore, as resulting from the mother's preoccupation with making ends meet, so to speak. For when it comes to dealing with the harshness of life, what takes priority is the reality of the experience, not the ideological source of it. Actually, if there is any "cultural" characteristic of the welfare subgroup, it is the constant frustration of the aspirations of its members rather than the provision of alternative ones. What we see among these women is not a relaxation of mores, not the development of a new code of moral rectitude, but rather the gradual emaciation of their security and hope and their slipping into an existence of unilateral dependence and socioeconomic irrelevance. I call this a state of existential emphraxis, brought about by societal dysfunctioning and livelihood exigencies.

Emphraxis--a Greek word whose American use has been limited so far to medicine--means the act of obstructing a passage from all possible directions: fencing in, stopping up, sealing in. The concept is very comprehensive because it implies both the obstruction as well as the deliberateness of it; both the process and the effect; the blocking force acting from without and the victim blocked within; the exercised pressure and the experienced impotence. The resort to emphraxis was made after fruitless effort to find an equally comprehensive concept in English. It is used here not only to indicate such barriers to employability as inadequate education and skills, lack of transportation, limited day-care facilities, poor health, but rather to describe the very results of these barriers and their original causes.

The reality of existential emphraxis forms the conceptual deduction of this study. The interviews with the women in Phoenix support the evidence presented in the literature that apparently WIN enrollees have incorporated the social values and share the cultural aspirations of American society. Their means of attaining them, however, have been thwarted by the stresses of their personal and social experiences.

Of course, this is not such a novel idea. After all, the whole war on poverty was fought on the principle that if situational barriers are removed, the poor will enter the mainstream of our society. The very WIN program was established on the premise that employment depends on the employability of the person, that is, on the individual's having the technical readiness and the physical capability for the job--a premise that at least implicitly accepts the existence of the work ethic among the welfare poor. What is the particular emphasis here is that technical and physical readiness are not the sole ingredients for success in the WIN program. Social and emotional ableness are just as basic requirements as they strongly affect a person's ability to perform.

The situational context of WIN families, therefore, merits equal attention in the planning of a training program. Again, the understanding is that the various personal and social disadvantages associated with chronic poverty have eroded the social capabilities of most AFDC recipients and have benumbed their defenses. Although voluntary enrollment in the WIN program and selective admission to it might indicate at least aspirational strengths and physical potential, still most enrollees are of fragile coping capacities in a social sense, due to the cumulative stress of their life space. Their vulnerability is continuously challenged by existing exigencies and recurrent pressures of their everyday life. The nitty-gritty of daily living may so intrude that they become dominant, overshadowing any other concern, especially involvements where there is a promise of only a questionable future, as the literature indicates is the case of the WIN training. The sense of "being trapped in a fate," the very essence of existential emphraxis, is not simply a state of mind but an active block-setter to the individual's self-actualization. When one feels so trapped, the promise of greater rewards at a later date for hard work seems quite "inoperative," to use a famous contemporary term.

Serving the Emphracted Client

From the above it is easy to postulate that all WIN enrollees are potential drop-outs. It is then the role of a manpower developing agency, serving thus emphracted individuals, to provide opportunities which will enable the enrollees to overcome not only the technical handicaps directly related with employability, but first those barriers which indirectly interfere with the enrollee's engagement in her employability plan. And this is the second conclusion drawn from this study.

Again, what is concluded here is not a startling revelation. Manpower programs of the sixties made it clear that the major target population was "the marginal part of the actual or potential labor force which suffer serious employability disadvantage in the primary labor market."[12] That is, the trend of manpower policies, of which WIN is a part, was not towards retraining the unemployed in newly-opened job areas, but toward leading those considered unemployable or, as is the fashionable term, the hard-to-employ. Mangum even suggests that "the main object of manpower policy and programs has to be those needing help in order to participate and perform effectively in the world of work."[13] However, all the above concerns focus on the low educational achievement, little skill, training and/or experience in employment, and other such disabilities that shortchange the "disadvantaged" in the competition of the private job market. On the other hand this study emphasizes a necessary first step of de-emphraxis, namely the allowance in the program for a process of revitalizing the resources of the enrollees before these resources can be tapped for training.

These emphracted women, as it was seen, live a way of life that provides them with a very narrow range of situations and expectations--the grocer, the landlady--a range that not only limits their knowledge of social roles but even beclouds their awareness of their actual standing. See, for instance, how enlightening and important the simple exercise of "mother's hats" was for the enrollees. The enrollees were not even aware of their significance to their own environment. On the contrary they were convinced of their own abject status and of the "failure" which it implies. What were the valued first steps were the changes in the content of interpersonal relations-- with training-mates, counselors--and the opportunity to participate in activities that took them out of the daily routine and into the world beyond the neighborhood. The valued result of these steps was the experience of testing one's own wings and seeing them gradually strengthening to the point of what Morris calls "functional independence,"[14] that is, the capacity to take care of one's own affairs to the extent that physical and economic conditions permit.

A collateral conclusion is that for the process of de-emphraxis to take place there must be an environment-- the organization, the agency and its staff in this case--that not only believes in the clients' capacity for change but actively recognizes their right to it; a generous environment that mobilizes all available resources--both in terms of skills and provisions--to meet the social, emotional, and concrete needs of the clients; an environment that is both protective and encouraging, both supportive and challenging. And most of all an environment that is free from ambiguity, confusion, and self-contradiction in its stated objectives and practicing policies. In other words it is the institutional structure of the delivery of services that will make the crucial difference in the outcome of a program like WIN. The WIN experiences were beneficial to the enrollees because the services given reflected the attitudes conveyed, the manner of help corresponded with the ideology of help and the objectives sought paralleled the promises made.

There still remains the question of why the Drop-Outs. Nothing in the study findings gives a clue as to a possible explanation. The simplest view would be to just say that among the "hard-to-reach" the Drop-Outs were the hardest. Or, as one enrollee said, "some people escaped help, too, you know." There is perhaps some validity to it in the sense that not all these women were at exactly the same level of social disablement, nor did they thaw out of their functional dependency in exactly the same pace. Yet, a reconsideration of the conclusions of this study forces an evaluation of the broader social welfare design of which WIN is a part.

According to the contingency theory,[15] an agency cannot deliver a better quality product than its larger system allows. As seen in the review of the literature, manpower policies have the dual goal of developing economic self-sufficiency and restoring functional self-sufficiency in individuals long considered outside the fringes of social institutions. However, given that economic self-sufficiency is primarily dependent upon economic and labor market considerations, far beyond the reach of human services programs, it is unrealistic to expect the meeting of both these objectives through the provision of social services alone, even if ample time is allowed and high level skills are guaranteed. A goal as dominated by economic forces as employment is, necessitates a multi-policy intervention of which the individual's preparation for employment is only a part. But if, on the other hand, the objective of the training agency is to assist the individual in reaching functional independence then, given adequate time and flexibility, the program is capable of altering the status of its enrollees regardless of their ultimate success in finding work. Considering the population served by such programs this is not a minor objective. As pointed out by O.E.C.D., its value "may be recognized both in terms of individual and family happiness and also in reduced risk of demands on health and welfare services."[16]

To return to the original question of why the Drop-Outs, perhaps what is needed is a reevaluation of the concept of success and a redefinition of the Success/Drop-Out proposition. In this we may borrow from the conviction of the enrollees--Successes and Drop-Outs alike--who have resolved for themselves that when WIN training "gets an individual to be his own decision maker, is success. Otherwise WIN is a failure."

The Broader Scope

The implications may be broader than this program assisting welfare mothers to reach functional independence. One of the noblest professional efforts in our times, one that nevertheless has created dilemmas and frustrations, has been the movement to deinstitutionalize chronic residents of mental institutions. Deinstitutionalization was based on the recognition that the mammoth institutions holding the mentally ill and mentally retarded were both costly and dehumanizing. In other words they created a different group of emphracted persons at a great expense to society. But deinstitutionalization is not a simple transfer of these people from one residence to another. The concept of deinstitutionalization, Scheerenberger points out, "involves an attitude, a principle and a complex process."[17] He explains that as an attitude, deinstitutionalization places great emphasis on an individual's independence, on his having the opportunity for personalized life experiences, mobility, and free interaction with others.[18] As a principle, deinstitutionalization clearly mandates the right of an individual to receive treatment in the least restrictive environment. This, too, addresses the individual's functional independence, his right to seek self-realization and become, as the WIN trainee said, "his own decision maker." Deinstitutionalization, like de-emphraxis, is a process, not a goal in itself. It is a complex process because the wrongs of the past must be undone first so that the individual can be brought back into the mainstream of society. The goal of deinstitutionalization[19] is "the increased independence and quality of life"[19] for the individual. This is the goal of de-emphraxis as well.

The lessons of WIN, thus, may be useful in setting developmental programs for those thrust into the community after long years of "sheltered," emphracted lives. They may also be of help in revamping our thinking about the way we respond to the needs of the disabled. Our policies towards the disabled, as Howard and his colleagues point out, have had the effect of "dichotomizing a continuum."[20] Whether suffering from chronic disabilities or experiencing a recent injury, whatever the nature of their impairment, the disabled have been viewed by the specification of our various programs, as being on either side of a dichotomy: disabled or nondisabled. For instance, decisions on disability benefits under Social Security are either to allow or to deny claims. "Considering that disability is a continuum, any point at which the line for dichotomy is drawn will leave doubtful cases on both sides."[21] Yet the International Social Security Association emphasized, as early as 1959,[22] that the role of social insurance is rehabilitation.[22] Our own concept of Social Security Disability Insurance did not address the need to provide employment as one of the policy's objectives. Instead, as Howard and his associates indicate, the disabled's inability to work was seen "as distinct from other forms of unemployment or under-employment."[23] As a result, the presence of expert witnesses--such as

140

physicians, social workers, lawyers--in claim adjudication hearings seems to be more significant to the outcome of the case than the case itself.[24]

The concept of emphraxis, with the process of rehabilitation it implies, could be significant in our responding more effectively and equitably to the needs of the disabled. Facing, as they do, financial, physical, and often emotional hardships, the disabled could be assisted in developing their own functional independence. The challenge there, as in WIN, is to individualize needs and provide opportunities for each person to maximize her/his own potential. This, after all, is what the disabled have declared as their due right.

It is obvious that the basic concepts of this study could be easily transferred to other groups and other situations. They are certainly applicable to other manpower training programs. This is particularly important in view of the current political mood to put an end to governmental indulgence. As "welfare" programs succumb to budgetary measures, attention is bound to turn to the development of human resources.

A Place for Advocacy

If nothing else this study reasserted that there are many factors that affect the performance of manpower programs and of the people engaged in them. Institutional sanctions, organizational constraints, environmental and attitudinal textures of the delivering agencies, and situational contexts of the clients all can and do, individually and synergistically, influence the outcome of a policy like the training of emphracted persons. We need, therefore, to intensify our efforts and inquiries into these factors if we are to develop effective approaches to the utilization of human potential. This plea aims beyond the customary call for further research in the recommendations section of a study like this one. Existential emphraxis, with all its ramifications, is a systematic situation that will respond only to systematic solutions. The development of relevant knowledge thus represents an imperative first step.

There still remains the question of how knowledge is utilized. There have been several evaluative efforts of manpower programs with concrete enough findings to suggest certain directions in policy. Yet, outcomes of social research have often been ignored and have been replaced by political considerations. Social policy directives have more often stemmed from ideologies than from analyses. Influence of such ideologies is not a negligible responsibility of the helping professional, not only in terms of asserting social values but also in terms of clarifying the activity that corresponds with such values.

In recent years, the concept of advocacy has gone far beyond the narrow role of legal advocate. Nonlegal advocacy has included assistance to various groups of people in gaining access to services and utilizing existing resources. It has been instrumental in influencing the social and political systems to become more responsive to identified needs. It has offered even encouragement and support to individuals to develop their own ability to advocate for themselves. Most importantly, the concept of advocacy involves the recognition that one of the worst disadvantages one can suffer is that of being excluded from the basic social institutions that form society.

Manpower planning, it is understood, is both a system of thought and a program for effective action. The decision to fit the hard-to-employ into productive jobs could be based on their need to work, or society's need for additional manpower, or the public's protest for selective idleness, but also on the societal value of one's right to work. It follows that appropriate policies are designed to support each decision. A commitment to full employment is a decision that implies the recognition of the value of work to the individual and of society's responsibility to make this value realizable by all. Such a decision has been reinforced in some countries with a philosophy of "an active manpower policy" as formulated by O.E.C.D. "Designed to reconcile and integrate the sometimes conflicting objectives of full employment, price stability, and rapid economic growth, active manpower policy stresses a variety of selective measures 'to supplement more permanent and general action' in order to 'create economic equilibrium while retaining full employment.'"[25] There are precedents of policies that are generous enough and flexible enough and which tend to the needs of those involved even when there is a long-seated and deep-rooted emphraxis that needs loosening. It is the social planner's responsibility to study these policies and promote them.

Planning for the Future

The need to plan appropriately must inevitably alert us to the direction of our society and to the need of considering it in our plans. We can no longer afford to plan in an "a la industrial revolution" style when we are soon to enter the twenty-first century. If it is true that present cultural values indicate more concern about the quality of life than quantity of goods; if work satisfaction is no longer just the result of a decent wage but rather of the opportunities for personal development and expression of creativity the job allows; if social participation is considered a human right, as is leisure and the opportunity for self-actualization: then human policies and the delivery of any human services must incorporate these "new vanguards"[26] in their provisions. This is not just ideological nobility, but reality testing pure and simple. The test of economic rationality, Topliss has pointed out, is the realization that societal responsibility for individual welfare must increase and must address broader aspects of the citizen's life. "This realization marks the development of the view that providing for the personal welfare of individuals is often not only compatible with, but conducive to, the economic and social well-being of the society as a whole."[27]

Successful intervention, therefore, must not only offset chronic disadvantages, but should also instill the security of one's entitlement to "the good life" if there is to be restored to the individual some measure of equality of opportunity to compete.

If WIN women--the subject of this speculation--are to enter the world of work force and stay in it, they must be prepared not only in marketable skills but also in attitudes of the present day workers. The emphracted individuals who form the WIN's population are in a sense in the same situation as the developing countries which must make the distance between their existential present to the twenty-first century in one big leap rather than in gradual steps. Human resources development programs must, therefore, anticipate in their provisions the consciousness raising and accelerated social expectations that "adjustment" to the world of work demands. In the case of women and members of ethnic minorities there should also be the anticipation of the new assertiveness that comes along with the need to perform in an "employment" capacity.

Modern social policy has espoused the principle that prevention is better than cure. However when dealing with existential emphraxis, the WIN experience has indicated that cure is what we must aim for. Nevertheless we may avoid a recycling of the "ailment" if we do not limit our service efforts to short-term goals but rather we project to further and more permanently-reaching program activities.

Such broad perspectives should also be maintained in the evaluation of the program. The means chosen to evaluate the program's performance are crucial as they will significantly influence the prescription for the program's treatment. The new developments in management technology and the identification of precise indicators for the measurement of program outcomes can be, and are, promising tools for planning. But when evaluating human services, the reliance on cost-benefit techniques alone could prove very misguiding and even detrimental to the very purposes of the program. The problem of evaluating human services is complex, but so is their nature. To quote Topliss again, "the real questions facing society today are not whether social legislation should in general have economic aims, but to what extent and in what areas of need, our society can afford to, and should ignore cost-benefit issues in promoting individual welfare."[28]

Europeans, Reubens reports, are "slow or resentful in establishing cost-benefit analysis of their program of hard-to-employ. . . . Implicitly, they have already placed such high values on human well-being, maintaining full employment, guaranteeing the right to work, and adding to the national output through the utilization of idle resources, that the benefits of rehabilitation or training, in general, must outweigh the costs."[29]

Again we are facing here the dilemma of value orientation. But a human orientation is not necessarily against technology. On the contrary, it suggests a discriminating use of technology and continuous effort to increase its discriminating efficiency. Perhaps it would be advisable to develop a model that employs multiple indices or multiple analytical activities where the impact of both short-term and long-term goals are assessed. In the meantime we must supplement existing measures with other tools of analysis and evaluation, or as Georgine Smith put it, "along

144

with a computer's view of the program we also maintain a people's view."[30]

The above recommendation places more responsibility on the professional. To counteract the difficulty of validly measuring the before-and-after impact of the service activity, the helping professional must be more clear and explicit about the specific needs of the client vis-a-vis the program provisions. "Giving everyone a chance" is a very humanitarian principle, but it may strongly conflict with a professional con-science if the agency and the program do not make the necessary allowances. It is important for the profes-sional to determine both what is possible within the framework of a policy as well as what is needed from the perspective of the client. The process of devel-oping an employability plan must be based not just on the enthusiasm and dedication of a worker but on a diagnosis of a client's potential and of the potential of the service apparatus; that is, on an informed decision that a client is employable if given basic manpower services, or can become employable if given special services along with the manpower training, or is not employable within the available provision of services, or cannot be employable even with the mobi-lization of all known services.

The Human Resources Specialist

The implementation of programs inevitably indicates contingencies not considered and engenders conflicts that must be resolved. Accountability lies with the helping professional not to make a virtue of necessity but to apply knowledge creatively, knowledge based on thorough theoretical and experiential constructs. Which brings us to what is needed in preparing profes-sionals to serve in manpower training programs and agencies.

On the basis of the findings of this study, the pri-mary objective of the helping relationship is to assist the client to restore, strengthen and maintain her self-respect, and revitalize her involvement in her self-improvement. That is nothing else than the old concept of promoting the client's abilities through the conscious use of self. Experience is needed in handling the range of difficulties likely to beset the client and in the range available to help her. Knowledge of societal factors, especially those

145

affecting occupational social welfare, as well as thorough understanding of behavioral considerations are also seen as basic to human resources specialists. However, beyond knowledge and skills there must be the professional's attitude about the client's right to improve her condition and to utilize all the available resources to realize this right.

A collateral attitude is the professional's conviction that the beneficiaries of human resources programs are not only the individual clients but the community and the larger society and that, therefore, her/his helping efforts should address macro-level issues, both economic and social. WIN has been a small program relative to the size and growth of the AFDC population. Should there be a large-scale public investment in job training, coupled with the kinds of support shown in the Phoenix WIN effort to have positive results, then these women could themselves seek social change and influence social welfare directions. The activities of National Association for Retarded Citizens, the dynamism of Grey Panthers, the accomplishments of Displaced Homemakers Network attest to the point.

As seen, the emphracted clientele of manpower programs like WIN requires a remedial approach on the part of both manpower and social welfare systems. In this sense WIN is one of the many social programs which link manpower development and social work. If the statement made in this study, that manpower development is based on the functional independence of the individuals involved, is valid, then there is an important role for social work in manpower programs.

Concluding Comments

This study has been an attempt to assess whether WIN supportive services are influential in an enrollee's engagement in her employability plan.

Despite some inconclusiveness in the data, there are important points that have been reasserted through this study. There has been substantial evidence which supports the common observation that the poor are kept from the labor force by multidimensional problems. Especially in the case of welfare women, this study has allowed for the clarification that such problems are rooted in the specific state of their life space.

This state has been identified as existential emphraxis, an existence circumscribed by a multitude of societal barriers and resulting handicaps. Plunged into the hold of existential emphraxis, these women need a system to connect them fully to their own potentialities. It thus becomes evident that dealing with the situational context of the enrollees is of primary importance to a manpower program for the disadvantaged, at least to the WIN program.

One cannot, on the basis of the findings, suggest that WIN I was an adequate program. But the study supports other findings that WIN appears capable of correcting the employment handicaps of most enrollees. However, the process takes time and requires careful activity. As it has already been stated, the activity must first be directed at counteracting the social atrophy that has resulted from the enrollee's emphracted state.

The findings do indicate some patterns of helpful activity when working with emphracted individuals. A basic element in this activity is that communication must take place on an emotional as well as semantic level. Also, it became evident that although self-determination is a prized concept, completely nondirective techniques prolong the restorative process and may even jeopardize it. Thus the responsibility falls on the helping professional to have not only the knowledge and technology but also the value orientation and commitment that would allow her/his engagement in the process of de-emphraxis.

There is a final point which I wish to emphasize. The concept of emphraxis is an optimistic one in that it suggests reversibility. It implies that the results of years of being disadvantaged can be overcome if given the proper attention. It thus opens the possibility for the development of policy and programs that would enable fuller utilization of human resources. It also alerts us to take precautional efforts to prevent the subjection of people to similar states. In a social service sense of a manpower training program, the concept of emphraxis suggests the overall concern of how to use the institution of work to improve the quality of life, to strengthen our human potential, and to contribute to a more just society. In a way this was the explicit intent of WIN I.

FOOTNOTES

CHAPTER VI

1. A. Smith, et al., "Win, Work and Welfare," op. cit., pp. 400-402. For a more extensive discussion of other studies see Chapter II, Part A.

2. G. Smith, Impact of Remedial and Supportive Services Upon Disadvantaged Job Applicants, op. cit., pp. 20-21.

3. D. L. Thompson and G. H. Miles, The Characteristics of the AFDC Population that Affect Their Success in WIN, op. cit., p. 62.

4. E. Opton, Factors Associated with Employment Among Welfare Mothers, op. cit., p. 197.

5. G. Mangum and R. T. Robson, eds., Metropolitan Impact of Manpower Programs: A Four-City Comparison (Salt Lake City: Olympus Publishing Company, 1973), p. 259.

6. See, for instance, John Holt, Why Children Fail (New York: Pitman Publishing Corporation, 1964).

7. J. Goldstein, The Effectiveness of Manpower Training Programs: A Review of Research on the Impact on the Poor, op. cit.

8. R. Perlman, Consumers and Social Services (New York: John Wiley and Sons, Inc., 1975), p. 19.

9. I. Howard, H. P. Brehn, and S. Z. Nagi, Disability. From Social Problem to Federal Program (New York: Praeger Publishers, 1980), p. 110.

10. R. Perlman, op. cit., p. 14.

11. Terms coined respectively by: O. Lewis, La Vida (New York: Random House, 1964) and D. Matza, "Poverty and Disrepute," in Contemporary Social Problems, R. K. Merton and R. Nisbet, eds. (New York: Harcourt, Brace and World, 1961).

12. R. Nixon, "Manpower--A New Area for Social Work and New Roles for Social Workers," in Manpower

and Employment, M. Purvine, ed. (New York: Council a Social Work Education, 1971), p. 259.

13. G. Mangum, The Emergence of Manpower Policy (New York: Rinehart and Winston, 1969), quoted in Nixon, ibid., footnote 2, p. 259.

14. R. Morris, "Welfare Reform 1973: The Social Service Dimension," Science, Vol. 181 (August 19, 1973), pp. 515-522.

15. P. R. Lawrence and J. W. Lorsch, Organization and Environment (Homewood, Ill.: Richard Irwin, 1969).

16. Organization for Economic Cooperation and Development, Promoting the Placement of Older Workers (Paris, 1967); quoted by B. G. Reubens, The Hard-to-Employ: European Programs, op. cit., p. 57.

17. R. Scheerenberger, Deinstitutionalization and Institutional Reform (Springfield, Ill.: Charles C. Thomas, 1976), p. 125.

18. Ibid., pp. 125-126.

19. Ibid., p. 177. Emphasis is the author's.

20. Howard, et al., op. cit., p. 121.

21. Ibid., p. 122.

22. I.S.S.A. Report IV, The Unification of the Basis for Measuring Impacts for Work (Geneva: Report of the XIIth General Meeting in London, May 12-22, 1958, 1959).

23. Howard, et al., p. 21.

24. Ibid., p. 122.

25. B. Reubens, op. cit., p. 32; quoting from O.E.C.D. reports and other sources.

26. Term coined by A. Gartner and F. Riessman, The Service Society and the Consumer Vanguard (New York: Harper and Row, 1974), p. 249. For an excellent discussion on value orientation and the world of work, see Work in America, Report of a

Special Task Force to the Secretary of HEW, op. cit.

27. E. Topliss, Provision for the Disabled (Oxford: Basil Blackwell, and London: Martin Robertson, 1975), p. 6.

28. Ibid., p. 10.

29. B. Reubens, op. cit., p. 39.

30. G. Smith, op. cit., p. 12.

APPENDIX A

151

Questionnaire for Enrollees

I. Listed below are some statements which describe possible experiences that a WIN enrollee might have had with the WIN personnel. During the various stages of your training you might have worked with one person only or with many. In answering the following questions, try to think in general of the person you worked with, the person "assigned" to you, so to speak. Please read each question carefully and check the answer that best describes your experience.

1. During the course of my contact with the WIN, I had the definite impression that the person assigned to me was:

   a. Definitely interested in helping me in all aspects of my life.

   b. Mostly interested in helping me to go through the program.

   c. Mainly interested in getting his/her work done.

   d. Definitely not interested in helping me.

2. While at the WIN I felt that the person assigned to me:

   a. Was deeply concerned that I become a happier person in every respect.

   b. Was deeply concerned that I become financially independent so that I can go off welfare.

   c. Was deeply concerned that I succeed in the program so that he/she has another success to his/her credit.

   d. Did not care at all whether I felt happy or not.

3. When I reported my problems to the WIN person assigned to me, he/she:

152

a. Accepted them as important and was able to assist me with them.

b. Accepted them as important and volunteered to help me if I needed any assistance.

c. Did not consider them serious enough to require his/her involvement.

d. Considered them insignificant.

4. Whenever I asked the WIN person assigned to me a question about his/her own life, he/she:

a. Answered the question simply and directly.

b. Avoided a direct answer but refocused on me.

c. Indicated that the question was not relevant to our work.

d. Answered grudgingly.

5. In times of trouble, the WIN person assigned to me:

a. Was sympathetic and practical in the solutions he/she suggested.

b. Was sympathetic and offered to help if I needed any assistance.

c. He/she told me what I should do.

d. Offered neither sympathy nor solutions.

6. Here is a made-up example. Let us say that one day you had car trouble and you telephoned to report that you could not go to the WIN office that day. What do you think the WIN person assigned to you would do:

a. Help you make possible arrangements so that you could go to the WIN office that day and/or in the future.

b. Suggest possible ways for you to go to the WIN office.

c. Insist that you find a way to go to the WIN office.

d. Express doubt about the truthfulness of your reason.

7. Another made-up example. Let us say you had trouble with your ex-husband, or sick children, or someone else in the family, and you were so upset that you could not do well in your training. What do you think the WIN person assigned to you would do:

a. Make it possible for you to continue attending the program while helping you handle your problem.

b. Sympathize with you and express understanding that you need to take some time off from the program so that you can handle your personal problems.

c. Insist that you must continue attending the WIN program because your training should have priority.

d. Question your motivation for training since you allow personal and family troubles to interfere with your work.

8. If one day you failed to show up in the WIN office the WIN person assigned to you would:

a. Call you to find out whether he/she could be of help.

b. Be interested enough to call and see what was the matter.

c. Call and complain about your failing to show up.

d. Not bother to call you.

9. If something in the way you looked (or behaved) could interfere with your preparing

for a job, the WIN person assigned to you would:

a. Help you make the needed changes.

b. Suggest that perhaps some changes are needed.

c. Tell you to change your appearance.

d. Criticize you about the way you look.

10. While you were at the WIN office, whenever you needed any assistance:

a. There was always someone available to help you.

b. There was usually someone around whom you could talk to.

c. You had to find someone from your team to talk to.

d. You had to wait until an appointment was scheduled for you with a team member.

II. The following are some statements regarding feelings which you might have or not have had when you enrolled in the WIN program. The possible answers are:

Strongly Agree
Somewhat Agree
Somewhat Disagree
Strongly Disagree

Please check the answer that best describes your feelings.

When I enrolled in the WIN program I felt that besides training I needed:

11. Emotional support because I was scared to go to work.

SA _____   SA _____   SD _____   SD _____

155

12. Help to stand on my own feet.

    SA _____   SA _____   SD _____   SD _____

13. To take some interest in my appearance.

    SA _____   SA _____   SD _____   SD _____

14. To learn how to schedule my day's work.

    SA _____   SA _____   SD _____   SD _____

15. Assistance with how to budget money.

    SA _____   SA _____   SD _____   SD _____

16. To build some confidence in myself.

    SA _____   SA _____   SD _____   SD _____

17. To learn to control my temper.

    SA _____   SA _____   SD _____   SD _____

18. To learn how to get along with people.

    SA _____   SA _____   SD _____   SD _____

19. Help with how to handle my children.

    SA _____   SA _____   SD _____   SD _____

20. To overcome my shyness.

    SA _____   SA _____   SD _____   SD _____

III. Here are some questions about the goals of the
WIN program. Again the choice of answers are:
Strongly Agree, Somewhat Agree, Somewhat Disagree, Strongly Disagree. Please check that
which best describes your ideas.

As you understand it, the WIN program was established in order to:

21. Give women on welfare another chance in life.

   SA _____ SA _____ SD _____ SD _____

22. Help welfare women become self-dependent.

   SA _____ SA _____ SD _____ SD _____

23. Primarily save the taxpayer money.

   SA _____ SA _____ SD _____ SD _____

24 Assist women on welfare get jobs of their choice.

   SA _____ SA _____ SD _____ SD _____

25. Force everyone to go to work.

   SA _____ SA _____ SD _____ SD _____

26. Make welfare women work for their keep.

   SA _____ SA _____ SD _____ SD _____

27. Help those who are able to move ahead in life.

   SA _____ SA _____ SD _____ SD _____

28. Make the government look good.

   SA _____ SA _____ SD _____ SD _____

29. Give welfare women the know-how of running their own lives.

   SA _____ SA _____ SD _____ SD _____

30. Provide cheap labor for the big business.

   SA _____ SA _____ SD _____ SD _____

IV. Following are some descriptions of possible conditions in a WIN office. Again there are four possible ways of responding: Strongly Agree, Somewhat Agree, Somewhat Disagree, Strongly Disagree. Please check the answer that best describes your impressions of the Phoenix office.

31. The WIN office was a really nice, friendly place.

    SA _____   SA _____   SD _____   SD _____

32. The WIN personnel treated the Enrollees as persons with special needs and interests.

    SA _____   SA _____   SD _____   SD _____

33. One could say that the general philosophy of the office was that strict rules do not guarantee efficiency.

    SA _____   SA _____   SD _____   SD _____

34. As the office was run, training was just one of the WIN experiences.

    SA _____   SA _____   SD _____   SD _____

35. People working there seemed relaxed doing their job.

    SA _____   SA _____   SD _____   SD _____

36. The consensus seemed to be that transportation of the Enrollee to and from the WIN office was an important factor of the WIN program and thus concerned Enrollees and staff alike.

    SA _____   SA _____   SD _____   SD _____

37. The primary concern of the WIN personnel was the general welfare of the Enrollee no matter what the consequences of the Enrollee's involvement with the program.

    SA _____   SA _____   SD _____   SD _____

38. The general procedure was to include the Enrollee's job interests in the selection of employability plans.

    SA _____   SA _____   SD _____   SD _____

39. The consensus seemed to be that first day-care arrangements were an important factor

for the WIN program and therefore concerned
Enrollees and staff alike.

SA _____ SA _____ SD _____ SD _____

40. The general philosophy was that primarily
the WIN office was a social service agency
rather than a training school.

SA _____ SA _____ SD _____ SD _____

APPENDIX B

Questionnaire for Staff

I. Listed below are some statements which describe possible experiences that a <u>WIN I</u> enrollee might have had with the WIN personnel. As a member of the staff of this WIN office, you have had contact with the enrollees and you are familiar with the services offered to them. On the basis of this knowledge you are asked to give <u>your perception</u> of these experiences. Please read each question carefully and check the answer that best describes your understanding of the possible experiences that the enrollee might have here.

1. During the course of an Enrollee's contact with the WIN, the Enrollee had the definite impression that the person assigned to her was:

   a. Definitely interested in helping the Enrollee in all aspects of her life.

   b. Mostly interested in helping the Enrollee to go through the program.

   c. Mostly interested in getting his/her work done.

   d. Definitely not interested in helping the Enrollee.

2. While at the WIN the enrollee felt that the person assigned to her:

   a. Was deeply concerned that the Enrollee become a happier person in every respect.

   b. Was deeply concerned that the Enrollee become financially independent so that she could go off welfare.

   c. Was deeply concerned that the Enrollee succeed in the program so that he/she has another success to his/her credit.

   d. Did not care at all whether the Enrollee felt happy or not.

162

3. When an Enrollee reported her problems to the WIN person assigned to her, he/she:

   a. Accepted them as important and was able to assist the Enrollee with them.

   b. Accepted them as important and volunteered to help the enrollee if she needed any assistance.

   c. Did not consider them serious enough to require his/her involvement.

   d. Considered them insignificant.

4. Whenever an Enrollee asked the WIN person assigned to her a question about his/her own life, he/she:

   a. Answered the question simply and directly.

   b. Avoided a direct answer but refocused on the Enrollee.

   c. Indicated that the question was not relevant to their work.

   d. Answered grudgingly.

5. In times of trouble, the WIN person assigned to the Enrollee:

   a. Was sympathetic and practical in the solutions he/she suggested.

   b. Was sympathetic and offered to help the Enrollee if she needed any assistance.

   c. He/she told the Enrollee what she should do.

   d. Offered neither sympathy nor solutions.

6. Here is a made-up example. Let us say that one day the Enrollee had car trouble and she telephoned to report that she could not go to the WIN office that day. What do you think the WIN person assigned to her would do:

a. Help the Enrollee make possible arrangements so that she could go to the WIN office that day and/or in the future.

b. Suggest possible ways for the Enrollee to go to the WIN office.

c. Insist that the Enrollee find a way to go to the WIN office.

d. Express doubt about the truthfulness of the Enrollee's reason.

7. Another made-up example. Let us say an Enrollee had trouble with her ex-husband, or sick children, or someone else in the family, and she was so upset that she could not do well in her training. What do you think the WIN person assigned to her would do:

a. Make it possible for the Enrollee to continue attending the program while helping her handle her problem.

b. Sympathize with the Enrollee and express understanding that she needs to take some time off from the program so that she can handle her personal problems.

c. Insist that the Enrollee must continue attending the WIN program because her training should have priority.

d. Question the Enrollee's motivation for training since she allows personal and family troubles to interfere with her work.

8. If one day an Enrollee failed to show up in the WIN office the WIN person assigned to her would:

a. Call the Enrollee to find out whether he/she could be of help.

b. Be interested enough to call and see what was the matter.

c. Call the Enrollee and complain about her failing to show up.

d. Not bother to call the Enrollee.

9. If something in the way an Enrollee looked (or behaved) could interfere with her preparing for a job, the WIN person assigned to her would:

    a. Help the Enrollee make the needed changes.

    b. Suggest to the Enrollee that perhaps some changes are needed.

    c. Tell the Enrollee to change her appearance (behavior).

    d. Criticize the Enrollee about the way she looked (behaved).

10. While at the WIN office, whenever an Enrollee needed any assistance:

    a. There was always someone available to help her.

    b. There was usually someone around whom an Enrollee could talk to.

    c. An Enrollee had to find someone from her team to talk to.

    d. An Enrollee had to wait until an appointment was scheduled for her with a team member.

II. The following are some statements regarding feelings which an Enrollee might, or might not have when she enrolls in the WIN program. The possible answers are:

> Strongly Agree
> Somewhat Agree
> Somewhat Disagree
> Strongly Disagree

Please check the answer that best describes the Enrollee feelings.

When a welfare recipient enrolled in the WIN program, I think that besides training she needs:

11. Emotional support because she is scared to go to work.

    SA _____ SA _____ SD _____ SD _____

12. Help to stand on her own feet.

    SA _____ SA _____ SD _____ SD _____

13. To take some interest in her appearance.

    SA _____ SA _____ SD _____ SD _____

14. To learn how to schedule her day's work.

    SA _____ SA _____ SD _____ SD _____

15. Assistance with how to budget money.

    SA _____ SA _____ SD _____ SD _____

16. To build some confidence in herself.

    SA _____ SA _____ SD _____ SD _____

17. To learn to control her temper.

    SA _____ SA _____ SD _____ SD _____

18. To learn how to get along with people.

    SA _____ SA _____ SD _____ SD _____

19. Help with how to handle her children.

    SA _____ SA _____ SD _____ SD _____

20. To overcome her shyness.

    SA _____ SA _____ SD _____ SD _____

III. Here are some questions about the goals of the WIN program. Again the choice of answers are: Strongly Agree, Somewhat Agree, Somewhat Disagree, Strongly Disagree. Please check that which best describes your ideas.

As you understand it, the WIN program was established in order to:

21. Give women on welfare another chance in life.

    SA _____ SA _____ SD _____ SD _____

22. Help welfare women become self-dependent.

    SA _____ SA _____ SD _____ SD _____

23. Primarily save the taxpayer money.

    SA _____ SA _____ SD _____ SD _____

24. Assist women on welfare get jobs of their choice.

    SA _____ SA _____ SD _____ SD _____

25. Force everyone to go to work.

    SA _____ SA _____ SD _____ SD _____

26. Make welfare women work for their keep.

    SA _____ SA _____ SD _____ SD _____

27. Help those who are able to move ahead in life.

    SA _____ SA _____ SD _____ SD _____

28. Make the government look good.

    SA _____ SA _____ SD _____ SD _____

29. Give welfare women the know-how of running their own lives.

    SA _____ SA _____ SD _____ SD _____

30. Provide cheap labor for the big business.

    SA _____ SA _____ SD _____ SD _____

IV. Following are some descriptions of possible conditions in a WIN office. Again there are four possible ways of responding: Strongly Agree, Somewhat Agree, Somewhat Disagree, Strongly Disagree. Please check the answer that best describes your impressions of the Phoenix office.

31. The WIN office was a really nice, friendly place.

   SA _____   SA _____   SD _____   SD _____

32. The WIN personnel treated the Enrollees as persons with special needs and interests.

   SA _____   SA _____   SD _____   SD _____

33. One could say that the general philosophy of the office was that strict rules do not guarantee efficiency.

   SA _____   SA _____   SD _____   SD _____

34. As the office was run, training was just one of the WIN experiences.

   SA _____   SA _____   SD _____   SD _____

35. People working here seemed relaxed doing their job.

   SA _____   SA _____   SD _____   SD _____

36. The consensus seemed to be that transportation of the Enrollee to and from the WIN office was an important factor of the WIN program and thus concerned Enrollees and staff alike.

   SA _____   SA _____   SD _____   SD _____

37. The primary concern of the WIN personnel was the general welfare of the Enrollee no matter what the consequences of the Enrollee's involvement with the program.

   SA _____   SA _____   SD _____   SD _____

38. The general procedure was to include the Enrollee's job interests in the selection of employability plans.

    SA _____ SA _____ SD _____ SD _____

39. The consensus seemed to be that the day-care arrangements were an important factor for the WIN program and therefore concerned Enrollees and staff alike.

    SA _____ SA _____ SD _____ SD _____

40. The general philosophy was that primarily the WIN office was a social service agency rather than a training school.

    SA _____ SA _____ SD _____ SD _____

BIBLIOGRAPHY

Aiken, Michael T., et al. <u>Coordinating Human Ser-</u>
<u>vices</u>. San Francisco: Jossey-Bass, 1975.

_____. <u>Economic Failure, Alienation, and Extrem-</u>
<u>ism</u>. Ann Arbor: The University of Michigan
Press, 1968.

Akabas, Sheila H., and Paul A. Kurzman, eds. <u>Work,</u>
<u>Workers and Work Organizations. A View From</u>
<u>Social Work</u>. Englewood Cliffs, NJ: Prentice-
Hall, Inc., 1982.

Albrow, Martin. <u>Bureaucracy</u>. New York: Praeger
Publishers Inc., 1970.

Allen, Vernon L. <u>Psychological Factors in Poverty</u>.
Chicago: Markham Publishing Company, 1970.

American Public Welfare Association Technical Assis-
tance Project. Reports: "Goals, Commitments,
Barriers, Propositions--Challenge to Validity,"
Chicago, 1967.

Andersen, Bent. <u>Work or Support</u>. Paris: Organization for Economic Cooperation and Development,
1966.

Anderson, Thomas P. "An Alternative Frame of Refer-
ence for Rehabilitation: The Helping Process
Versus the Medical Model." In <u>The Psychological</u>
<u>and Social Impact of Physical Disability</u>. Eds.
R. P. Marinelli and A. E. Delt Orto. New York:
Springer Publishing Company, 1977, pp. 17-24.

Appel, Gary Louis. <u>Effects of a Financial Incentive</u>
<u>on AFDC Employment: Michigan's Experience Be-</u>
<u>tween July 1969 and July 1970</u>. Minneapolis:
Institute for Interdisciplinary Studies, 1972.

Arizona Blue Book 1971-1972, A Guide to the State of
Arizona, Arizona State Library Association.

<u>Arizona Poverty Profile</u>, 1980. Phoenix: Human Devel-
opment Council Diocese of Phoenix, 1980.

Aronson, Robert L. <u>The Localization of Federal Man-</u>
<u>power Planning</u>. Ithaca, NY: Cornell University,
1973.

Atkinson, John, and Norman Feather. A Theory of Achievement Motivation. New York: John Wiley and Sons, 1966.

Auerbach Associates. An Impact Evaluation of the Work Incentive Program. Philadelphia: Auerbach Associates (September 15, 1972).

Azzi, Corry F. Equity and Efficiency Effects from Manpower Programs. Lexington: Lexington Books, 1973.

Bakke, Wright E. Citizens Without Work. New Haven: Archon Books Edition, 1969.

_____. The Unemployed Man. London: Nisbet and Co., Ltd., 1933.

Bandura, Albert. Principles of Behavior Modification. New York: Holt, Reinhart and Winston, 1969.

Banfield, Edward. The Unheavenly City. Boston: Little, Brown and Company, 1970.

Barsby, Steve L. Cost-Benefit Analysis and Manpower Programs. Lexington, Mass.: Lexington Books, D. C. Heath and Company, 1972.

Bateman, Worth. "Assessing Program Effectiveness." Welfare in Review, Vol. 6, No. 1 (January-February 1968), pp. 1-10.

Bell, Daniel. The Coming of Post-Industrial Society: A Venture in Social Forecasting. New York: Basic Books, 1973.

Benn, Stanley I., and Richard S. Peters. Social Principles and the Democratic State. London: Allen University, 1959.

Bennett, Marianne, and Robert P. McNeill. "Advocacy." In Planning for Services to Handicapped Persons, Community, Education, Health. Eds. Phyllis R. Magrab and Jerry O. Elder. Baltimore: Paul H. Brookes, 1979, pp. 173-191.

Bentrup, Walter C. "The Profession and the Means Test." Social Work, Vol. 9, No. 2 (April 1964), pp. 10-17.

Berkowtz, Monroe, et al. Rehabilitating Social Security Disability Insurance Beneficiaries: The Promise and the Performance. New Brunswick, NJ: Rutgers University Bureau of Economic Research, 1978.

Berlin, G. "Jobs or Welfare: A Look at Programs for Female Heads of Households." County Employment Reporter, Vol. 7, No. 4 (August), pp. 11-16.

Bernard, Sidney E. The Economic and Social Adjustment of Low-Income Female-Headed Families. Unpublished Dissertation, Brandeis University, May 1964.

Birney, Robert, et al. Fear of Failure. New York: Van Nostrand-Reinhold Company, 1969.

Blau, Peter M. "Orientation Toward Clients in a Public Welfare Agency." In Social Welfare Institutions. Ed. Mayer N. Zald. New York: John Wiley & Sons, Inc., 1965, pp. 654-670.

_____ and W. Richard Scott. Formal Organizations: A Comparative Approach. San Francisco: Chandler Publishing Company, 1962.

Blaxter, Mildred. The Meaning of Disability. London: Heinman Educational Books Limited, 1976.

Bluestone, Barry. "Economic Theory and the Fate of the Poor." Social Policy, Vol. 2, No. 5 (January-February 1972), pp. 30-31, 46-48.

Bolino, August C. Manpower and the City. Cambridge, Mass.: Schenkman Publishing Company, 1969.

Borgatta, Edgar F., et al. Social Workers' Perceptions of Clients. New York: Russell Sage Foundation, 1960.

Borus, Michael E., and William R. Tash. Measuring the Impact of Manpower Programs: A Primer. Ann Arbor: Institute of Labor and Industrial Relations, 1970.

Briar, Scott. "Welfare from Below: Recipients' Views of the Public Welfare System." In The Law of the Poor. Ed. Jacobus TenBroek. San Francisco: Chandler Publishing Company, 1966, pp. 44-61.

_____ and Henry Miller. <u>Problems and Issues in Social Casework</u>. New York: Columbia University Press, 1971.

Brown, J. Douglas. <u>An American Philosophy of Social Security: Evolution and Issues</u>. Princeton, NJ: Princeton University Press, 1972.

Brozen, Yale. "Toward an Ultimate Solution." <u>Saturday Review</u> (May 23, 1970), pp. 30-31, 60-61.

Burke, Vee, and Alair A. Townsend. <u>Public Welfare and Work Incentives: Theory and Practice</u>. Studies in Public Welfare, Paper No. 14, Subcommittee on Fiscal Policy, Washington, DC: U.S. Government Printing Office, 1974.

Burns, Eveline M. "What's Wrong with Public Welfare." <u>Social Service Review</u>, Vol. 36, No. 2 (June 1962), pp. 111-122.

Burnside, Betty. "The Employment Potential of AFDC Mothers in Six States." <u>Welfare in Review</u>, Vol. 9, No. 4 (July-August 1971), pp. 16-20.

Cain, Glen G. <u>Married Women in the Labor Force, An Economic Analysis</u>. Chicago: University of Chicago Press, 1966.

_____ and Robinson G. Hollister. "Evaluating Manpower Programs for the Disadvantaged." <u>Cost-Benefit Analysis of Manpower Policies</u>. In <u>Proceedings of a North American Conference</u>. Eds. G. G. Somers and W. D. Wood. Ontario: Industrial Relations Center, Queen's University at Kingston, 1969.

Campbell, Donald, and Donald Fiske. "Convergent and Discriminant Validation by the Multitrait-Multimethod Matrix." <u>Psychological Bulletin</u>, Vol. 56, No. 2 (March 1959), pp. 81-104.

Cantril, Hadley. <u>The Pattern of Human Concerns</u>. New Brunswick, NJ: Rutgers University Press, 1965.

Carter, Genevieve. "The Challenge of Accountability-- How We Measure the Outcomes of Our Efforts." <u>Public Welfare</u>, Vol. 29, No. 3 (Summer 1971), pp. 267-277.

_____. "The Employment Potential of AFDC Mothers." Welfare in Review, Vol. 6, No. 4 (July-August 1968), pp. 1-11.

Cartwright, Desmond, et al. "Method Factors in Changes Associated with Psychotherapy." Journal of Abnormal Social Psychology, Vol. 66, No. 2 (February 1963), pp. 164-175.

Chadwin, Michael L. WIN Federal Management System. Washington, DC: The Urban Institute, 1979.

Clegg, Reed K. The Welfare World. Springfield, Ill.: Charles C. Thomas, 1968.

Cloward, Richard A., and Lloyd E. Ohlin. Delinquency and Opportunity. New York: The Free Press, 1960.

Cohen, Julius S., et al. Vocational Rehabilitation and the Socially Disabled. Syracuse, NY: Syracuse University Press, 1966.

Cohen, Wilbur, J., et al. "Social Security Act Amendments of 1954: A Summary and Legislative History." Social Security Bulletin, Vol. 17, No. 9 (September 1954), pp. 3-18.

Collins, Alice H. The Lonely and Afraid. New York: The Odyssey Press, 1969.

Committee for Economic Development. Training and Jobs for the Urban Poor--A Statement of National Policy. New York: 1970.

Coser, Lewis A. "The Sociology of Poverty." Social Problems, Vol. 13, No. 2 (Fall 1965), pp. 141-148.

Cox, Irene. "The Employment of Mothers as a Means of Family Support." Welfare in Review, Vol. 8, No. 6 (November-December 1970), pp. 9-17.

Cumming, Elaine. Systems of Social Regulation. New York: Atherton Press, 1968.

Delehanty, John, ed. Manpower Problems and Policies. Scranton, PA: International Textbook Company, 1969.

175

Denitch, Bogdan. "Is There a 'New Working Class?' A Brief Note on a Large Question." In The Worker in "Post Industrial" Capitalism. Eds. Bertram Silverman and Murray Yanowitch. New York: The Free Press, 1974, pp. 175-179.

Deshaies, Dennis J. "A Client-Centered Manpower Perspective." In The Production of Manpower Specialists. Ed. John R. Niland. Ithaca, NY: New York State School of Industrial and Labor Relations, 1971, 160-167.

Downs, Anthony. Who Are the Poor?, Supplementary Paper Number 26 (rev. ed.). New York: Committee for Economic Development, 1970.

Dubey, Sumati N., et al. "Structural Factors in Noncompliance in Referring Clients to Programs in a Large Public Welfare Agency," The WIN Research Project: Preliminary Report. School of Applied Social Sciences--Case Western Reserve University, Cleveland, Ohio: August, 1970. (Mimeographed.)

Dunning, Bruce B. Posttraining Outcomes: Experiences with the Portland WIN Voucher Training Program. Washington, DC: Bureau of Social Science Research, Inc., 1977.

Durbin, Elizabeth F. Welfare Income and Employment. New York: Frederick A. Praeger, 1969.

Ehrenberg, Ronald B., and James G. Hewlett. The Impact of the WIN 2 Program on Welfare Costs and Recipient Rates. Technical Analysis Paper No. 15-C. Washington, DC: U.S. Department of Labor, 1975. (Draft.)

Eklund, E. Systems Advocacy. Lawrence, KS: Kansas University Affiliated Facility, University of Kansas, 1976.

Elder, Jerr O. "Coordination of Service Delivery Systems." In Planning for Services to Handicapped Persons, Community, Education, Health. Eds. Phyllis R. Magrab and Jerry O. Elder. Baltimore: Paul H. Brooks, 1979, pp. 193-209.

Elman, Richard M. "If You Were on Welfare." Saturday Review (May 23, 1970), pp. 27-29, 61.

_____. _The Poorhouse State_. New York: Pantheon Books, 1966.

Entis, Elliot Z. _An Organizational Analysis of WIN Separate Administrative Units_. Washington, DC: REAP Associates, Inc., 1979. (Forthcoming.)

Eppley, David B. "The AFDC Family in the 1960's." _Welfare in Review_, Vol. 8, No. 5 (September-October 1970), pp. 8-16.

Erlanger, Howard S., et al. _Disability Policy: The Parts and the Whole_. Discussion paper, Institute for Research on Poverty, University of Wisconsin, 1979.

Esterly, Stanley, and Glenn Esterly. _Freedom from Dependence_. Washington, DC: Public Affairs Press, 1971.

Eyde, Lorraine Dittrich. _Work Values and Background Factors as Predictors of Women's Desire to Work_. Research Monograph No. 108--Bureau of Business Research, The Ohio State University, Columbus, 1962.

Farb, T. _Unified Planning and Funding in the Work Incentive Program: A Review of Implementation_. Washington, DC: National Institute of Public Management, 1978.

Feagin, Joe R. "American Welfare Stereotypes." _Social Science Quarterly_, Vol. 52, No. 4 (March 1972), pp. 921-933.

Federal Poverty Programs: Assessment and Recommendations. The Institute for Defense Analyses, Report R-116. Arlington, VA: The Institute for Defense Analyses, 1966.

Fenderson, Douglas Allen. _A Study of the Vocational Rehabilitation Potential of Applicants for Social Security Disability Benefits Whose Claims Have Been Denied_. Ann Arbor: University Micro Films, 1966.

Ferman, Louis A. _Job Development for the Hard-to-Employ_. Policy Papers in Human Resources and Industrial Relations, No. 11, A Joint Publication of the Institute of Labor and Industrial Rela-

177

tions of University of Michigan and Wayne State University and the West Virginia University, 1969.

_____. "Some Perspectives on Evaluating Social Welfare Programs." The Annals of the American Academy of Political and Social Sciences, Vol. 385 (September 1969), pp. 143-156.

Fine, Ronald E., et al. Final Report: AFDC Employment and Referral Guidelines. Minneapolis: Institute for Interdisciplinary Studies--Welfare Policy Division (June 30, 1972).

Franklin, David. A Longitudinal Study of WIN Dropouts: Program and Policy Implications. Los Angeles: Regional Research Institute in Social Welfare--University of Southern California, 1972.

Friedlander, Frank, and Stuart Greenberg. "The Effect of Job Attitudes Training and Organization Climate Upon Performance of the Hard-Core Unemployed." Journal of Applied Psychology, Vol. 55, No. 4 (1971), pp. 287-295.

Friedman, Lawrence M. "Social Welfare Legislation: An Introduction." Stanford Law Review, Vol. 21, No. 1 (January 1969), pp. 217-247.

Friedrich, Carl F. "Some Observations on Weber's Analysis of Bureaucracy." Reader in Bureaucracy. Ed. Robert K. Merton. Glencoe: The Free Press, 1952, pp. 27-33.

Frohlich, Phillip. Denied Disability Insurance Applicants: A Comparison with Beneficiaries and Nonapplicants. Washington, DC: Social Security Administration, Division of Disability Studies, Office of Research and Statistics, 1970.

Furniss, Norman, and Timothy Tilton. The Case for the Welfare State: From Social Security to Social Equality. Bloomington: Indiana University Press, 1977.

Gabor, Dennis. "Fighting Existential Nausea." Technology and Human Values. Santa Barbara: Center for the Study of Democratic Institutions, 1966.

Gans, Herbert. The Urban Villagers. Glencoe: The Free Press, 1962.

_____. "Urban Poverty and Social Planning." In The Uses of Sociology. Eds. F. Paul Lazarsfeld, et al. New York: Basic Books, 1967, pp. 437-476.

Ganter, G. Yeakel, and Norman Polansky. Retrieval from Limbo. New York: Child Welfare League of America, 1967.

Garfinkel, Irwin. How Income Supplements Can Affect Work Behavior. Studies in Public Welfare, Paper No. 13, Subcommittee on Fiscal Policy. Washington, DC: U.S. Government Printing Office, 1974.

Gartner, Alan, and Frank Riessman. The Service Society and the Consumer Vanguard. New York: Harper and Row, 1974.

Gartner, Alan, et al., eds. Public Service Employment. New York: Praeger, 1973.

Garvin, Charles D., ed. Incentives and Disincentives to Participation in the Work Incentive Program. Ann Arbor: The University of Michigan School of Social Work, 1974.

German, Peral S., and Joseph W. Collins. Disability and Work Adjustment. Washington, DC: Social Security Administration, Division of Disability Studies, Office of Research and Statistics, 1974.

Ginzberg, Eli, and Herbert A. Smith. Manpower Strategy for Developing Countries--Lessons from Ethiopia. New York: Columbia University Press, 1967.

Gold, Stephen S. "Comment: The Failure of the Work Incentive (WIN) Program." University of Pennsylvania Law Review, Vol. 119, No. 3 (January 1971), pp. 485-501.

Goldberg, Richard. "Vocational Rehabilitation of Patients on Long-Term Hemodialysis." Archives of Physical Medicine and Rehabilitation, Vol. 55, No. 2, (February 1974), pp. 60-64.

Golding, George, et al. Psychodynamics and Enablement in the Rehabilitation of the Poverty-Bound

Client. Lexington, MA: Heath Lexington Books, 1970.

Goldstein, Jon H. The Effectiveness of Manpower Training Programs: A Review of Research on the Impact on the Poor. Studies in Public Welfare, Paper No. 3, Subcommittee on Fiscal Policy. Washington, DC: U.S. Government Printing Office, 1972.

Goodwin, Leonard. A Study of the Work Orientations of the Welfare Recipients Eligible for and Partici- pating in the Work Incentive Program: A Report on First Phase Results. Washington, DC: The Brookings Institution, 1971.

_____. Do the Poor Want to Work? Washington, DC: The Brookings Institution, 1972.

Gottsfeld, Harry. "Professionals and Delinquents Evaluate Professional Methods with Delinquents." Social Problems, Vol. 13, No. 1 (Summer 1965), pp. 45-59.

Gouldner, Alvin W. "Organizational Analysis." In Sociology Today. Eds. Robert K. Merton, et al. New York: Basic Books, 1959, pp. 400-428.

_____. "The Norm of Reciprocity: A Preliminary Statement." American Sociological Review, Vol. 25, No. 2 (April 1960), pp. 161-178.

Green, Christopher. "Negative Taxes and Monetary Incentives to Work: The Static Theory." Journal of Human Resources, Vol. 3, No. 3 (Summer 1968), pp. 280-288.

Green, C., and A. Tella. "Effects of Nonemployment Income and Wage Rates on the Work Incentive of the Poor." Review of Economics and Statistics, Vol. 51, No. 4 (November 1969), pp. 339-408.

Greene, Leonard. Free Enterprise Without Poverty. New York: W. W. Norton and Company, Inc., 1981.

Greenwood, Ernest. Experimental Sociology, A Study in Method. New York: King's Crown Press, 1945.

Greer, Colin. The Great School Legend. New York: Basic Books, 1972.

Gursslin, Orvill R., and Jack L. Roach. "Some Issues in Training the Unemployed." Social Problems, Vol. 12, No. 1 (Summer 1964), pp. 86-98.

Halmos, Paul. The Faith of the Counselors. A Study in the Theory of Practice of Social Case Work and Psychotherapy. New York: Schocken Books, 1966.

Hamilton, John A. "Will 'Work' Work?" Saturday Review (May 23, 1970), pp. 24-27.

Hampden-Turner, Charles. From Poverty to Dignity: A Strategy for Poor Americans. Garden City, NY: Anchor Press/Doubleday, 1974.

Handler, Joel F., and Ellen Jane Hollingsworth. Work and the Aid to Families with Dependent Children. Discussion papers, Institute for Research on Poverty. Madison: The University of Wisconsin, 1969.

_____. "Work, Welfare, and the Nixon Reform Proposals." Stanford Law Review, Vol. 22, No. 5 (May 1970), pp. 907-942.

Hanoch, Giora. "An Economic Analysis of Earnings and Schooling." Journal of Human Resources, Vol. 2, No. 3 (Summer 1967), pp. 310-329.

Hansen, H. Morris, and Genevieve W. Carter. "Assessing Effectiveness of Methods for Meeting Social and Economic Needs." In Economic Progress and Social Welfare. Ed. Leonard H. Goodman. New York: Columbia University Press (published for N.C.S.W.), 1966, pp. 92-124.

Hardin, Einar, and Michael E. Borus. The Economic Benefits and Costs of Retraining. Lexington, MA: Heath Lexington Books, 1971.

Hargrove, Erwin C. The Missing Link: The Study of the Implementation of Social Policy. Washington, DC: The Urban Institute, 1978.

Harrington, Michael. The Other America: Poverty in the United States. New York: Macmillan, 1963.

Hausman, Leonard J. The Potential for Work Among Welfare Parents. Manpower Research Monograph No.

12. Washington, DC: U.S. Government Printing Office, 1969.

Haveman, Robert H. "Public Employment of Less Productive Workers: Lesson for the United States from the Dutch Experience." In Disability Policies and Government Programs. Ed. Edward D. Berkowitz. New York: Praeger Publishers, 1979.

Having the Power, We Have the Duty. Report of the Advisory Council on Public Welfare to the Secretary of Health, Education, and Welfare. Washington, DC: U.S. Government Printing Office, 1966.

Heilbroner, Robert L. "Economic Problems of a 'Post-industrial' Society." Dissent, Vol. 20, No. 2 (Spring 1973), pp. 163-176.

Heins, James A. "The Negative Income Tax, Head Grants, and Public Employment Programs: A Welfare Analysis." The Journal of Human Resources, Vol. 5, No. 3 (Summer 1970), pp. 298-303.

Hines, Joseph S. "Some Work-Related Cultural Deprivation of Lower-Class Negro Youth." Journal of Marriage and the Family, Vol. 26, No. 1 (January 1964), pp. 447-49.

Hoffman, Lois Wladis, and F. Ivan Nye. Working Mothers. San Francisco: Jossey-Bass Publishers, 1974.

Hokenson, Earl, et al. Incentives and Disincentives in the Work Incentive Program. Minneapolis: Interstudy, 1976. (Final Report.)

Hollis, Florence. Casework. A Psychosocial Therapy. New York: Random House, 1965.

Holt, John C. How Children Fail. New York: Pitman Publishing Corporation, 1964.

Hoos, Ida R. Retraining the Work Force. Berkeley: University of California Press, 1967.

Hostetler, Zona Fairbanks. "Poverty and the Law." In Poverty as a Public Issue. Ed. Ben B. Seligman. New York: The Free Press, 1965, pp. 177-230.

Howard, Irving, et al. DISABILITY: From Social Problem to Federal Program. New York: Praeger Publishers, 1980.

"Inside Phoenix '72." Yearly report published by The Arizona Republic and The Phoenix Gazette.

International Social Study Association. Report IV: The Unification of the Basis for Measuring Incapacity for Work. Geneva: Report of the XIIth General Meeting in London (May 12-22, 1958), 1959.

Jahoda, Marie, et al. Marienthal--The Sociography of an Unemployed Community. Chicago and New York: Aldine-Atherton, Inc., 1971.

_____. Research Methods in Social Relations, Parts 1 and 2. New York: The Dryden Press, 1951.

Joe, Tom. "Rethinking Welfare Strategy." Congressional Record (March 5, 1973), pp. 1369-1373.

Johnson, W. G., and E. Murphy. "The Response of Low Income Households to Income Losses from Disability." Industrial and Labor Relations Review, Vol. 29, No. 1 (October 1975), pp. 85-96.

Jones, Peter. "Rights, Welfare and Stigma." In Social Welfare: Why and How? Ed. Noel Timms. London, Boston and Henley: Routledge and Kegan Paul, 1980, pp. 123-144.

Kaitz, Edward M., and Herbert H. Hyman. Urban Planning for Social Welfare, A Model Cities Approach. New York (Washington and London): Praeger Publishers, 1970, Praeger Special Studies in U.S. Economic and Social Development.

Kasper, Hirshchel. "Welfare Payments and Work Incentive: Some Determinants of the Rates of General Assistance Payments." The Journal of Human Resources, Vol. 3, No. 1 (Winter 1968), pp. 86-110.

Katona, George, et al. Aspirations and Affluence, Comparative Studies in the United States and Western Europe. New York: McGraw-Hill, 1971.

Katz, Elihu, and S. N. Eisenstadt. "Bureaucracy and Its Clientele--A Case Study." In Readings in

Modern Organizations. Ed. Amitai Etzioni. Englewood Cliffs: Prentice-Hall, Inc., 1969.

Keniston, Kenneth. The Uncommitted. Alienated Youth in American Society. New York: Dell Publishing Co., Inc., 1960.

Kershaw, Joseph. Government Against Poverty. Chicago: Markham Publishing Company, 1970.

Kessler, Henry H. Disability--Determination and Evaluation. Philadelphia: Lea and Febger, 1970.

Killingsworth, Charles C. "Automation, Jobs and Manpower." In Poverty in America. Ed. Louis A. Ferman, et al. Ann Arbor: University of Michigan Press, 1965, pp. 259-273.

Kir-Stimon, William. Discards on Trial. Chicago: Rehabilitation Institute of Chicago (June), 1963.

Klausner, Samuel Z. The Work Incentive Program: Making Adults Economically Independent. Philadelphia: University of Pennsylvania, 1972.

Knupfer, Genevieve. "The Poverty-Stricken State of Mind." In Contemporary Society. Ed. Jackson Toby. New York: John Wiley and Sons, 1964.

Korpi, Walter. "Approaches to the Study of Poverty in the United States" Critical Notes from a European Perspective." In Poverty and Public Policy. An Evaluation of Social Science Research, Ed. Vincent Covello. Cambridge, MA: Schenkman Publishing Company, 1980, pp. 287-314.

Krusen, Edward, and Dorothy E. Ford. "Compensation Factor in Low Back Injuries." The Journal of the American Medical Association. Vol. 166, No. 10 (March 8, 1958), pp. 1128-1133.

Kuhn, Manford H. "The Interview and the Professional Relationship." In Human Behavior and Social Process. Ed. Arnold M. Rose. Boston: Houghton Mifflin, 1962, pp. 193-205.

Langer, Thomas, et al. "Psychiatric Impairment in Welfare and Nonwelfare Children." Welfare in Review, Vol. 7, No. 2 (March-April 1969), pp. 10-21.

Levine, Abraham S. "Cost-Benefit Analysis and Social Welfare--An Exploration of Possible Applications." Welfare in Review, Vol. 4, No. 2 (February 1966), pp. 1-11.

Levine, Robert E. The Poor Ye Need Not Have with You: Lessons from the War on Poverty. Cambridge: M.I.T. Press, 1970.

Levinson, Perry. "How Employable are AFDC Women." Welfare in Review, Vol. 8, No. 4 (July-August 1970), pp. 12-16.

Levison, Andrew. The Working-Class Majority. New York and Baltimore: Penquin Books, Inc., 1975.

Levitan, Sar A., and William B. Johnston. Work is Here to Stay, Alas. Salt Lake City: Olympus Publishing Company, 1973.

Levitan, Sar A., and Garth L. Mangum. Federal Training and Work Programs in the Sixties. Ann Arbor: Institute of Labor and Industrial Relations Publication, 1969.

Levitan, Sar A., and Robert Taggart, III. Employment and Earnings Inadequacy: A New Social Indicator. Baltimore: Johns Hopkins University Press, 1974.

_____. Jobs for the Disabled. Baltimore: Johns Hopkins University Press, 1977.

_____. Social Experimentation and Manpower Policy: The Rhetoric and the Reality. Baltimore: Johns Hopkins University Press, 1971.

_____. The Promise of Greatness. Cambridge, MA: Howard University Press, 1976.

Levitan, Sar A., et al. Work and Welfare Go Together. Baltimore: Johns Hopkins University Press, 1972.

Liebow, Elliot. Tally's Corner. Boston: Little, Brown, 1967.

Lynde, John M. "Trends in AFDC Recipients, 1961-1965." Welfare in Review, Vol. 5, No. 5 (May 1967), pp. 7-14.

Macarov, David. Incentives to Work. San Francisco: Jossey-Bass, Inc., 1970.

MacIver, Robert Morrison. The Ramparts We Guard. New York: Macmillan, 1950.

Mangum, Garth L. Contributions and Costs of Manpower Development and Training, Policy Papers in Human Resources and Industrial Relations, No. 5. Ann Arbor and Detroit: The Institute of Labor and Industrial Relations, December 1967.

_____. "Determining the Results of Manpower and Antipoverty Programs." The Analysis and Evaluation of Public Expenditures: The PPB System, Vol. 3, Joint Economic Committee, Washington, DC, 1969, pp. 1174-1175.

_____ and David Snedeker. Manpower Planning for Local Labor Markets. Salt Lake City: Olympus Publishing Company, 1974.

_____ and R. Thayne Robson, eds. Metropolitan Impact of Manpower Programs: A Four-City Comparison. Salt Lake City: Olympus Publishing Company, 1973.

Marshall, Alfred. Principles of Economics. London: Macmillan, 1966.

Marsden, Dennis. Mothers Alone. Poverty and the Fatherless Family. London: Allen Lane, the Penguin Press, 1969.

Maslow, Abraham H. Motivation and Personality. New York: Harper and Brothers, 1954.

Matza, David. "Poverty and Disrepute." In Contemporary Social Problems. Eds. R. K. Merton and R. Nisbet. New York: Harcourt, Brace and World, 1961.

Mayer, John E., and Noel Timms. The Client Speaks. New York: Atherton Press, 1970.

McKinlay, John B. "Some Approaches and Problems in the Study of the Use of Services--An Overview." Journal of Health and Social Behavior, Vol. 13, No. 2 (June 1972).

186

Merton, Robert K. <u>Social Theory and Social Structure</u>, rev ed. London: The Free Press of Glencoe, 1964.

Mikkelson, Edwin J. "The Psychology of Disability." <u>Psychiatric Annals</u>, Vol. 7, No. 2 (February 1977), pp. 90-100.

Miller, Henry. "Characteristics of AFDC Families." <u>Social Service Review</u>, Vol. 39, No. 4 (December 1964), pp. 399-409.

Miller, Herman P. <u>Rich Man Poor Man</u>. New York: Crowell, 1971.

Miller, Joyce. "New Focus on the Handicapped." <u>American Federationist</u>, AFL-CIO, Vol. 85, No. 1 (January 1978), pp. 17-20.

Miller, S. M. "Education and Jobs: Lessons of the '60's." <u>Social Policy</u>, Vol. 2, No. 5 (January-February 1972), pp. 43-45.

_____ and Frank Riessman. <u>Social Class and Social Policy</u>. New York: Basic Books, 1968.

_____ and Martin Rein. "Poverty, Inequality and Policy." In <u>Social Problems: A Modern Approach</u>. Ed. H. Becher. New York: Wiley and Sons, 1966.

Mischel, Walter. <u>Personality and Assessment</u>. New York: John Wiley and Sons, Inc., 1968.

Morris, Robert. "Welfare Reform 1973: The Social Service Dimension." <u>Science</u>, 181 (August 10, 1973), pp. 515-522.

Morrison, Donald M. "Is the Work Ethic Going Out of Style?" <u>Time</u> (October 31, 1972), pp. 96-97.

Morton, Malvin, ed. <u>Can Public Welfare Keep Pace?</u> New York: Columbia University Press, 1969.

Moynihan, Daniel. "One Step We Must Take." <u>Saturday Review</u> (May 23, 1970), pp. 20-23.

Myrdal, Gunnar. <u>Asian Drama</u>. New York: Pantheon, 1968.

Nixon, George. People, Evaluation and Achievement. Houston: Gulf Publishing Company, 1973.

Nixon, Russell. "Manpower--A New Area for Social Work and New Roles for Social Workers." In Manpower and Employment. Ed. Margaret Purvine. New York: Council on Social Work Education, 1971, pp. 257-267.

O'Connor, Robert, and Julian Rappaport. "Application of Social Learning Principles to the Training of Ghetto Blacks." American Psychologist, Vol. 25, No. 7 (July 1970), pp. 659-661.

Oetting, E. R., et al. Intervening to Improve Work Adjustment of the Disadvantaged. Vol. 7, Final Report, Experimental Manpower Laboratory, Colorado State University. Fort Collins, Colorado, 1974. (Mimeographed.)

_____. Work and the Disadvantaged. Vol. 1, Final Report, Summary Volume Experimental Manpower Laboratory, Colorado State University. Fort Collins, Colorado, 1974. (Mimeographed.)

Ogren, Evelyn. "When a Recipient Organization Provides Social Services." Welfare in Review, Vol. 9, No. 2 (March-April 1971), pp. 14-22.

Olmstead, Joseph. Organizational Structure and Climate: Implications for Agencies. Working Papers No. 2, Department of HEW, Social and Rehabilitation Service (February 1973).

Opton, Edward M., Jr. Factors Associated with Employment Among Welfare Mothers. Berkeley: The Wright Institute, 1971.

Orcutt, Guy H., and Alice G. Orcutt. "Incentive and Disincentive Experimentation for Income Maintenance Policy Purposes." American Economic Review, Vol. 58, No. 4 (September 1968), pp. 754-772.

Orr, Larry, et al., eds. Income Maintenance: Interdisciplinary Approaches to Research. Chicago: Markham, 1971.

O'Toole, James, ed. Work and the Quality of Life. Cambridge, MA: The M.I.T. Press, 1974.

Parsons, Talcott. Essays in Sociological Theory, rev.
ed. New York: The Free Press, 1966.

_____. Structure and Process in Modern Society.
Glencoe: The Free Press, 1960.

Perlman, Robert. Consumers and Social Services. New
York: John Wiley & Sons, Inc., 1975.

Perrucci, Robert. "Work in the Cybernetic State."
The Triple Revolution Emerging. In Social Problems in Depth. Eds. Robert Perrucci and Marc
Pilisuk. Boston: Little, Brown and Company,
1971.

Piven, Frances Fox, and Richard A. Cloward. Regulating the Poor. New York: Pantheon Books, 1971.

Polanyi, Karl. The Great Transformation. Boston:
Beacon Press, 1944.

Pollock, K., and S. Geams. Preliminary Findings of a
Study of the Effects of the WIN and Welfare Employment Tax Credits. Minneapolis: Institute
for Manpower Program Analysis, Consultation and
Training, 1976.

Prescott, Edward, et al. "Training and Employability:
The Effect of MDTA on AFDC Recipients." Welfare
in Review, Vol. 9, No. 1 (January-February 1971),
pp. 1-6.

Prien, Erich, P., et al. Mental Health in Organization: Personal Adjustment and Constructive Intervention. Chicago: Nelson-Hall, 1979.

Pruger, Robert, and Charles Wilder. Poverty, Concep-
tions, Reality, Issues. New York: MSS Modular
Publications, Inc., Module 24 (1974), pp. 1-26.

Query, William T. Illness, Work and Poverty. San
Francisco: Jossey-Bass, Inc., 1968.

Rainwater, Lee. What Money Buys: Inequality and the
Social Meanings of Income. New York: Basic
Books, 1974.

Ragg, Nicholas. "Respect for Persons and Social Work:
Social Work as 'Doing Philosophy.'" In Social
Welfare: Why and How? Ed. Noel Timms. London,

189

Boston and Henley: Routledge and Kegan Paul, 1980, pp. 211-232.

Reid, William J., ed. Decision-Making in the Work Incentive Program. Chicago: School of Social Services Administration, University of Chicago, 1972.

_____ and Ann W. Shyne. Brief and Extended Casework. New York: Columbia University Press, 1969.

_____ and Audrey D. Smith. "AFDC Mothers View the Work Incentive Program." The Social Service Review, Vol. 46, No. 3 (September 1972, pp. 347-362.

Rein, Martin. "Social Policy Analysis as the Interpretation of Beliefs." Journal of the American Institute of Planners, Vol. 37, No. 5 (September 1971), pp. 297-310.

_____. Social Policy. Issues of Choice and Change. New York: Random House, 1970.

Rein, Mildred. Work or Welfare? Factors in the Choice of AFDC Mothers. New York: Praeger Publishers, 1974.

_____ and Barbara Wishnov. "Patterns of Work and Welfare in AFDC." Welfare in Review, Vol. 9, No. 6 (1971), pp. 7-12.

Reubens, Beatrice. The Hard-to-Employ: European Programs. New York: Columbia University Press, 1970.

Ribich, Thomas J. Education and Poverty. Washington, DC: The Brookings Institution, 1968.

Rickard, Thomas E., et al. "Indices of Employer Prejudice Toward Disabled Persons." In Social and Psychological Aspects of Disability. Ed. Joseph Stubbins. Baltimore: University Park Press, 1977, pp. 523-529.

Riessman, Frank. "Quantum Leap or More Foreplay for the Human Services." Social Policy, Vol. 2, No. 5 (January-February 1972), pp. 3-4.

Ripley, Randall B. "Legislative Bargaining and the Food Stamps Act, 1964," Congress and Urban Problems. Washington, DC: The Brookings Institution, 1969.

Ripple, Lilian, et al. Motivation, Capacity and Opportunity. Social Service Monographs, The School of Social Service Administration, University of Chicago, 1964.

Roder, Frank S. "Why Work?" The Journal of Public Social Services, Vol. 2, No. 1 (March 1971), pp. 1-5.

Rodman, Hyman. "Illegitimacy in the Carribean Social Structure: A Reconsideration." American Sociological Review, Vol. 31, No. 5 (October 1966), pp. 673-683.

Roe, D. Physical Rehabilitation and Employment of AFDC Recipients. Ithaca, NY: Cornell University, 1975.

Roessner, J. David. Employment Context and Disadvantaged Workers. Washington, DC: Bureau of Social Science Research, Inc., November 1971.

Rosenberg, Morris. "Faith in People and Success-Orientation." In The Language of Social Research. Eds. Paul F. Lazarsfeld and Morris Rosenberg. New York: The Free Press, 1955, pp. 158-161.

Rosenheim, Margaret K. "Vagrancy Concepts in Welfare Law." In The Law of the Poor. Ed. Jacobus TenBroek. San Francisco: Chandler Publishing Company, 1966, pp. 187-242.

Sacks, Joel G., et al. Clients' Progress Within Five Interviews. New York: Family Service Association of America, 1970.

Safilios-Rothschild, Constantina. The Sociology and Social Psychology of Disability and Rehabilitation. New York: Random House, 1970.

_____. "Women and Work: Policy Implications and Prospects for the Future." In Women Working. Eds. Ann H. Stromberg and Shirley Harkness. Palo

Alto, CA: Mayfield Publishing Company, 1978,
pp. 419-432.

Scheerenberger, R. C.   Deinstitutionalization and
Institutional Refocus. Springfield, IL: Charles
C. Thomas, 1976.

Scherberg, Goldie. The Work Ethic. Paper presented
at the 50th Annual Meeting of American Orthopsychiatric Association, New York (June 1, 1973).
(Mimeographed.)

Schiller, Bradley R. The Impact of Urban WIN Programs. Washington, DC: Pacific Training and
Technical Assistance Corporation, 1972.

_____. The Pay-Off to Job Search: The Experience
of WIN Terminees. Washington, DC: Pacific
Training and Technical Assistance Corporation,
1974.

_____, et al. The Impact of WIN II: A Longitudi-
nal Evaluation. Washington, DC: Pacific Consultants, 1976.

Schorr, Alvin L. Explorations in Social Policy. New
York and London: Basic Books, 1968.

_____. "People, Not Slogans." Social Work, Vol.
17, No. 2 (March 1972), p. 2.

Schultz, Theodore W. "Investment in Human Capital."
American Economic Review, Vol. 51, No. 1 (March,
1961), pp. 1-17.

Sear, B. N. Reentry of Women to the Labour Market
After an Interruption in Employment. Organiza-
tion for Economic Cooperation and Development,
Paris, 1971.

Seligman, Ben B. Permanent Poverty: An American
Syndrome. Chicago: Quadrangle Books, 1970.

Sewell, D. O. Training the Poor: A Benefit-Cost
Analysis of Manpower Programs in the U.S. Anti-
poverty Program. Industrial Relations Centre,
Queens University, Kingston, Ontario, 1971.

Shatz, Eunice O., and Sheldon S. Steinberg. The WIN
Program--An Appraisal. Paper presented at 98th

Annual Forum, National Conference on Social Welfare, Dallas, May 17, 1971. (Mimeographed.)

Sheppard, Harold L., et al., eds. The Political Economy of Public Service Employment. Lexington, MA: Lexington Books, 1972.

Shorter, Edward, ed. Work and Community in the West. New York: Harper and Row, 1973.

Siegel, Irving, ed. Manpower Tomorrow: Prospects and Priorities. New York: Augustus M. Kelley, 1967.

Silverman, Phyllis R. "The Client Who Drops Out: A Study of Spoiled Helping Relationships." Unpublished PhD dissertation, Florence Heller Graduate School for Advanced Studies in Social Welfare, Brandeis University, 1968.

Simmons, Harold E. Work Relief to Rehabilitation. Sacramento: The Citadel Press, Inc., 1969.

Sinsheimer, Robert B. "The Existential Casework Relationship." Casework, Vol. 50, No. 2 (February 1969), pp. 67-73.

Skolnick, Jerome H., and Elliott Currie, eds. Crisis in American Institutions. Boston: Little, Brown and Company, 1970.

Smarr, Erwin R., and Philip J. Escoll. Humanism and the American Work Ethic. A Psycho-Social Perspective. Paper presented at the 50th Annual Meeting of American Orthopsychiatric Association, New York, June 1, 1973. (Mimeographed.)

Smith, Audrey D., et al. After WIN: A Follow-up Study of Participants of the Work Incentive Program. Chicago: Center for the Study of Welfare Policy, School of Social Service Administration, University of Chicago, 1975.

_____. "WIN, Work and Welfare." Social Service Review, Vol. 49, No. 3 (September 1975), pp. 396-404.

Smith, Georgine. Impact of Remedial and Supportive Services Upon Disadvantaged Job Applicants. Research Section, Institute of Management and Labor

Relations. Rutgers: State University of New Jersey, June 1971.

Smith, Vernon. Welfare Work Incentives. The Earnings Exemption and Its Impact upon AFDC Employment, Earnings and Program Cost. Lansing, Michigan: Department of Social Services, 1974.

_____ and Aydin Ulysan. The Employment of AFDC Recipients in Michigan, Studies in Welfare Poli- cy. Lansing, Michigan: Department of Social Services, 1972.

Somers, Gerald G., ed. Retraining the Unemployed. Madison: University of Wisconsin Press, 1968.

Specht, Harry. "The Deprofessionalization of Social Work." Social Work, Vol. 17, No. 2 (March 1972), pp. 5-15.

Spencer, Michael L., and Jan L. Stephen. "An Alter- native to Do-Nothingness." Journal of Public Social Services, Vol. 1, No. 4 (December 1970), pp. 24-27.

Spradley, James. You Owe Yourself a Drunk. Boston: Little, Brown, 1970.

Stein, Bruno, and S. M. Miller. Incentives and Plan- ning in Social Policy. Chicago: Aldine Publish- ing Company, 1973.

Stein, Robert L. "The Economic Status of Families Headed by Women." Monthly Labor Review, Vol. 93, No. 12 (1970), pp. 3-10.

Stevens, Robert B., ed. Income Security, Statutory History of the United States. New York, Toronto, London, Sydney: Chelsea House Publishers (in association with McGraw-Hill Book Co.), 1970.

Strathy, Ester, et al. The Role of the Social Worker in a Day-Care Center. Paper presented at the 50th Annual Meeting of the American Orthopsychi- atric Association, New York, June 1, 1973. (Mimeographed.)

Stromsdorfer, Ernst W. "Determinants of Economic success in Retraining the Unemployed." Journal

of Human Resources, Vol. 3, No. 2 (Spring, 1968),
pp. 139-158.

Sussman, Marvin. "Dependent Disabled and Dependent
Poor: Similarity and Conceptual Issues and Re-
search Needs." In Social and Psychological
Aspects of Disability. Ed. Joseph Stubbins.
Baltimore: University Park Press, 1979, pp. 247-
259.

_____, ed. Sociology and Rehabilitation. Washing-
ton, DC: American Sociological Association,
1966.

TenBroek, Jacobus. "California's Dual System of Family Law: Its Origin, Development and Present
Status." Stanford Law Review, Vol. 16 (March
1964), pp. 257-317; Vol. 16 (July 1964), pp. 900-
981; Vol. 17 (April 1965), pp. 614-682.

Therkildsen, Paul T. Public Assistance and American
Values. Albuquerque: University of New Mexico,
1964.

Thoenes, Piet. The Elite in the Welfare State. New
York: The Free Press, 1966.

Thomas, Edwin J. "Problems of Disability from the
Perspective of Role Theory." In Behavioral Sci-
ences for Social Workers. Ed. Edwin J. Thomas.
New York: The Free Press, 1967, pp. 59-77.

Topliss, Eda. Provision for the Disabled. Oxford:
Basil Blackwell; London: Martin Robertson, 1975.

Udy, Stanley. "'Bureaucracy' and 'Rationality' in
Weber's Organization Theory." American Sociological Review, Vol. 24, No. 6 (December 1959), pp.
791-795.

U.S. Department of Labor. Implementing Welfare-Employment Programs: An Institutional Analysis of the
Work Incentive (WIN) Program. R & D Monograph
78, Employment and Training Administration, 1980.

U.S. Department of Labor. "WIN Program Data, Table
18: Cumulative Enrollments and Termination and
Current Enrollment by Region, State and Project
as of 2/28/71." Manpower Administration, Office

of Manpower Management, Data Systems, Division of Reports Analysis, Washington, DC, 1971.

U.S. Department of Labor. Manpower Report of the President. Washington, DC: U.S. Government Printing Office, 1974.

U.S. Department of Labor. The Work Incentive (WIN) Program and Related Experience. R & D Monograph 49, Employment and Training Administration, 1977.

U.S. Senate, Finance Committee. Social Security Amendments of 1971. CIS (1971 S361-10.3), pp. 128-186.

Valley National Bank. Arizona Statistical Review. 28th Annual Edition, September 1972.

Vinter, Robert D. "Analysis of Treatment Organizations." In Behavioral Sciences for Social Workers. Ed. Edwin J. Thomas. New York: The Free Press, 1967, pp. 207-221.

Wadel, Cato. Now, Whose Fault is That? The Struggle for Self-Esteem in the Face of Chronic Unemployment. Newfoundland Social and Economic Studies, No. 11. Toronto: University of Toronto Press, 1973.

Wattenberg, Ester. "Learned Helplessness: Women in the Labor Force." The Social Welfare Forum, 1974, Proceedings of 101st Annual Forum, National Conference on Social Welfare. New York: Columbia University Press, 1975.

W. E. Upjohn Institute for Employment Research. Work in America. Report of a special task force to the Secretary of Health, Education and Welfare. Cambridge, MA: The M.I.T. Press, 1973.

Weber, Max. "Bureaucracy." From Max Weber: Essays in Sociology, eds. H. H. Gerty and C. Wright Mills. London and New York: Oxford University Press, 1946.

_____. "The Essentials of Bureaucratic Organizations." In Reader in Bureaucracy. Ed. Robert K. Merton. Glencoe: The Free Press, 1952, pp. 18-27.

Weinberger, Paul E. _Perspectives on Social Welfare._ London: The Macmillan Company (Collier-Macmillan, Ltd.), 1969.

Weiner, Hyman J., et al. _Mental Health Care in the World of Work._ New York: Association Press, 1973.

Weisbrod, Burton A. "Conceptual Issues in Evaluating Training Programs." _Monthly Labor Review,_ Vol. 89, No. 10 (October 1966), pp. 1091-1097.

_____. "Education and Investment in Human Capital." _Journal of Political Economy,_ Vol. 70, No. 1 (Supplement, October 1962), pp. 106-123.

_____. "Investing in Human Capital." _Journal of Human Resources,_ Vol. 1, No. 1 (Summer 1966), pp. 5-21.

"The Welfare and Child Health Provisions of the Social Security Amendments of 1967." _Welfare in Review,_ Vol. 6, No. 3 (May-June 1968), pp. 1-34.

Wiseman, Michael. _Change, Turnover in a Welfare Population._ Berkley: University of California, Department of Economics, 1976.

"Who Will Do the Dirty Work?" _Fortune,_ Vol. 89, No. 1 (January 1974), 132ff.

WIN Handbook. Operational Procedures for the Work Incentive Program. Arizona State Employment Service, July 1968.

WIN--Technical Assistance Handbook. Prepared by the Office of Human Resources Development and Training Operations of the U.S. Employment Service, November 1968.

Wogaman, Philip J. _Guaranteed Annual Income: The Moral Issues._ Nashville: Abingdon Press, 1968.

Wool, Harold. "What's Wrong with Work in America?--A Review Essay." _Monthly Labor Review,_ Vol. 96, No. 3 (March 1973), pp. 39-43.

Worby, Marsha. "The Adolescent's Expectations of How the Potentially Helpful Person Will Act." _Smith_

College Studies in Social Work, 26 (1955), pp. 19-59.

The Work Incentive Program. Fourth Annual Report to the Congress, Committee on Ways and Means. Washington, DC: U.S. Government Printing Office, 1974.

Working Papers No. 1.   National Study of Social Welfare and Rehabilitation Workers, Work, and Organizational Contexts.   Department of Health, Education and Welfare, Social and Rehabilitation Service (SRS-ORD-177), May 1971.

Working Papers No. 2.   "Organizational Structure and Climate: Implications for Agencies."   National Study of Social Welfare and Rehabilitation Workers, Work, and Organizational Contexts, Department of Health, Education and Welfare, Social and Rehabilitation Service (73-05403), February 1973.

Zald, Mayer N. Occupations and Organizations in American Society.   Chicago: Markham Publishing Company, 1971.

Zimpel, Lloyd, and Daniel Panger.   Business and the Hardcore Unemployed.   New York: Frederick Fell, Inc., 1970.

Office of Economic Opportunity, 27
Organizational issues, 44-47; behavior, 45;
  goals, 46
Organization of Economic Planning &
  Development, 138, 141

Poor law, 35
Poverty: culture of, 134; socio-psychological
  consequences of, 39-42
Problem preception & identification, 132-133
Productivity, 29-30

Ridit, 39
Rotter I-E test, 70

Service delivery, 5-6, 42-44
Services: counseling qualitites, 70, 126-127;
  evaluation of human, 143; social, 42-44;
  supportive WIN 4, 42-44, 63-65, 126;
  barriers to treatment, 42-44
Social planning, 142
Social Security Act, 2; 1967 amendments, 2;
  Talmadge Amendments 1971, 5, 7, 23, 74
Stigma, 40
Substitution effect, 35
Supply system, 28

Taylor Manifest Anxiety Scale, 70
Training programs, 43

Vacuum effect, 55
Vagrancy and laws, 32

Wages, 28; minimum, 28; levels, 113
Welfare, 26-27; AFDC, 37-40; public
  assistance 25, 27, 39, 46, 47;
  policy, 25-28, 33; caseloads, 29, 32
Welfarization, 37; welfarized, 37
Work, 33-34; "orientations", 16-17;
  incentives, 33
Work-fare, 2, 32, 37; legislation, 2

Author Index